Praise for *In Her Own Voice*

"I've spent most of my career observing and studying the forces and skills that allow people to move from individual contributor to influential and powerful leader. When I read *In Her Own Voice*, I was thrilled to learn that Jennifer provides a playbook for a successful journey to leadership that will inspire and enlighten any woman who is ready to undertake the challenging but very rewarding journey to transformational leadership. Using your authenticity as your competitive advantage, your experience to drive your confidence, and your relationships as leverage, this book will punctuate your journey. Read it, embrace it and go get 'em!"

—Carla Harris, Senior Client Advisor at Morgan Stanley
and best-selling author of *Expect to Win*

"Inspiring! Giving a voice to women around the world, Jennifer McCollum's new book shines a light on the critical areas for businesses to support and develop women, while also helping women to overcome their obstacles for advancement. Insightful and backed by relevant research, *In Her Own Voice* provides the tools for everyone to become an advocate and champion for women in business today."

—Marshall Goldsmith, *New York Times* best-selling author of
The Earned Life, *Triggers*, and *What Got You Here Won't Get You There*

"The beauty of this book is that it's based on the experiences of tens of thousands of women, with guidance that is applicable to every one of us, no matter where we are on our own unique journey. The caring candor found in these pages is reflective of what happens—and can happen—in real life. I wish that I had the voices and experiences of these women at my side when I was progressing through my career."

—Anne Chow, former CEO of AT&T Business, Lead Director at
FranklinCovey, and member of the Board of Directors at 3M

"*In Her Own Voice* is one of the most clearheaded and least grandiose books I have read about the future of work post-pandemic. It highlights the key role women must play in helping companies meet the challenge of an empowered and highly diverse workforce that demands an inclusive environment in which they feel recognized and valued. And it lays out how women can address both external and internal impediments in order to assume this role. A must-read for any woman who's ready to rise . . . and for any company ready to support her in that ascent."

—Sally Helgesen, best-selling author of *How Women Rise*,
Rising Together, and *The Female Advantage*

"Jennifer McCollum has drawn a road map to help women gain clarity on what they want, take risks that create recognized confidence, manage their leadership brand, and operate successfully with increasing authenticity. All women who aspire to leadership should read this book—and so should the senior leaders who can make a difference as sponsors."

—Herminia Ibarra, The Charles Handy Professor of Organisational Behaviour at the London Business School and author of *Act Like a Leader, Think Like a Leader* and *Working Identity: Unconventional Strategies for Reinventing Your Career*

"I've been a friend and mentor of Jennifer's since 2020, when she approached and asked me to help her apply principles of my 'Working Together© Leadership and Management System and Culture of Love by Design' at Linkage. I was privileged to be a part of helping the organization navigate the challenges of COVID-19 and emerge stronger on the other side. This book provides a glimpse at the brainpower (and heart-power) of the woman at the helm of that turnaround."

—Alan Mulally, former CEO of Ford Motor Company and Boeing Commercial Airplanes, and member of the Board of Directors at Google (now Alphabet), Carbon 3D, and the Mayo Clinic

"As intersectionality is increasingly discussed, more companies are seeking to understand how our multiple, interlocked identities—woman of color, member of the LGBTQIA+ community, person with a disability—shape how we experience the world. Books like *In Her Own Voice* can help. While the main 'voice' is Jennifer McCollum's, she's careful to include stories and quotes from women of various races, backgrounds, and orientations who've climbed to positions of power. The more we understand the intersecting identities and experiences of all women, the better off our organizations will be."

—Marilu Galvez, President and General Manager at WABC-TV New York and Emmy Award–winning journalist

"It's my pay-it-forward mission to add more executive-level women on public and private boards, and that's how Jennifer McCollum and I intersected. We share the conviction that more gender-diverse boards will accelerate a shift of more gender-diverse corporate leadership teams. We're making strides in the boardroom arena, and the best companies are following suit to get more women in their C-suite. *In Her Own Voice* is a great starting point. Whether you're a senior leader looking for a way to support talented women, or an individual who's serious about moving up in the ranks, you'll love the compelling stories and practical advice in this book."

—Maggie Wilderotter, former CEO and Executive Chairman of Frontier Communications; Board Member of Costco Wholesale Corporation, Lyft, and Sana Biotechnology; and Board Chair at DocuSign

"What makes a person influential has little to do with working harder or having the most impressive skills. It's more about our ability to view messy problems as opportunities, act boldly amid uncertainty, and adapt to the unwritten rules. McCollum's research and stories demonstrate how women become impact players and influential leaders. Aspiring C-suiters, take notice: *In Her Own Voice* is the voice of wisdom and will guide you on your ascent."

—Liz Wiseman, CEO of The Wiseman Group and *New York Times* best-selling author of *Multipliers* and *Impact Players*

"As a sports agent for almost two decades, I had a front-row seat to peak performance. I saw the difference between the ones who make it to the top and stay there, and the ones who don't and why. Those who sustained success had a drive to get better every single day. This is also true in the quest for leadership in business. With a data-grounded road map, Jennifer McCollum helps women crack the code on what it will take to accelerate faster into leadership ranks, and what organizations can do to support them. A must-read for women and men at any level who care about the future of work."

—Molly Fletcher, author of *The Energy Clock* and host of the *Game Changers with Molly Fletcher* podcast

"We're all immersed in busy-ness. The upside is we get the status hit that comes with being important, and perhaps the credit for being a hardworking employee. The downside is we get mired in the short-term-thinking quicksand that prevents us from doing the strategic thinking, planning, and relationship-building it takes to play the long game. Every page of this book convinces me that Jennifer McCollum knows how to play the game right. She has crafted a life that's not just successful but meaningful and deeply fulfilling. And here's the thing: so can you."

—Dorie Clark, *Wall Street Journal* best-selling author of *The Long Game* and executive education faculty, Columbia Business School

IN HER OWN VOICE

A Woman's Rise to CEO

Overcoming Hurdles to Change the Face of Leadership

JENNIFER McCOLLUM

Matt Holt Books
An Imprint of BenBella Books, Inc.
Dallas, TX

Matt Holt is an imprint of BenBella Books, Inc.
10440 N. Central Expressway
Suite 800
Dallas, TX 75231
benbellabooks.com
Send feedback to feedback@benbellabooks.com

BenBella and *Matt Holt* are federally registered trademarks.

Printed in the United States of America
10 9 8 7 6 5 4 3 2 1

Library of Congress Control Number: 2023012882
ISBN 9781637744109 (hardcover)
ISBN 9781637744116 (electronic)

Editing by Katie Dickman
Copyediting by Lydia Choi
Proofreading by Marissa Wold Uhrina and Jenny Bridges
Text design and composition by PerfecType, Nashville, TN
Cover design by Brigid Pearson
Printed by Lake Book Manufacturing

Special discounts for bulk sales are available. Please contact bulkorders@benbellabooks.com.

To my father, Roy Scherer, who believed well before
I did that I had a story worth telling.

To my mother, Sandy Baker,
who always encouraged whatever I envisioned.

To my husband, Chip McCollum,
who supports my dreams unconditionally.

To my children, Madeleine, Will, and Hunter,
who are my greatest teachers.

CONTENTS

PART THREE
ELIMINATING THE HURDLES

A NOTE FROM THE SHRM CEO

Johnny C. Taylor, Jr.

This is a book whose time has come.

As the CEO of SHRM, I have a unique vantage point. I engage daily with HR leaders and business executives to track what's happening in the world of work—across time, sectors, and geography. The changes that have taken place in the past few years are nothing less than staggering.

For all the suffering and heartbreak caused by COVID-19, it brought things into sharp focus for many people. It caused us to reevaluate what we wanted with our life and our work.

There's a collective sense of urgency to create more human-centric workplaces where all employees—both women and men—can grow and thrive. Women, too, have undergone a profound mindset shift; no longer are they willing to sit back and hope for the best. This is their moment—and they're seizing it.

In Her Own Voice is the perfect book for this inflection point in history.

For women, it does a beautiful job of explaining not just what to do to advance in your career, but also what to expect. For leaders, it helps you recognize the gap between what you think women seeking advancement want and what they really need.

For HR professionals, it shows you what good looks like. For men, it shows us how to be advocates and part of the solution.

Jennifer McCollum is the right person to tell this story. She is a premier thought leader, and I had the privilege of meeting her in 2022, when she was CEO of Linkage and SHRM acquired the company.

Linkage is known for the depth and breadth of its research on leadership, and that shines through in this book. Jennifer has done a great job of synthesizing this storehouse of knowledge and connecting it to tactics that are practical, concise, and contemporized for the world we live in. Also, she masterfully weaves in stories—her own and those of other women—that bring the lessons to life.

Not only has Jennifer walked the walk, but she's also curious and driven to learn from others. She is on a quest for knowledge and has a passion and expertise about women in leadership that aligns with our SHRM vision—to build a world of work that works for all.

Jennifer wrote this book because she wants to have a serious impact on women in the workforce who, like her, wish to lead, influence, and inspire others. It is the culmination of a lifetime of hard work, experience, and wisdom.

This partnership with Jennifer and Linkage has been an amazing experience. I believe together our two organizations have the power to create a game-changing journey for women everywhere.

I hope *In Her Own Voice* means as much to you as it does to me. In these pages I hear not only Jennifer's voice but the voices of all women who long to share their gifts with the world.

FOREWORD

Anne Chow

CEO. It's a title that explicitly holds a respectful degree of gravitas and a role that implicitly represents a breadth of responsibilities spanning a company's full purview. Historically, this position has been held by men across countless industries. In today's modern world, perhaps naively so, I didn't realize how unique becoming a woman CEO actually was—until I became one.

In the early days of my corporate career, which spanned over three decades working for a Fortune 15 company, I had an inkling that leadership was in my future. Interactions between people have always fascinated me, and I was intrigued by how organizational dynamics worked in the context of delivering impact. In my first several roles as an individual contributor traversing network engineering, international operations, and product management, I had an opportunity to work for and with both female and male leaders. I observed many women working hard to fit in—whether in the way they dressed, carried themselves, asserted their voices, or interacted with others. This was in the 1990s, and I remember my impression that one had to be extroverted, strong, and forceful, while presenting a more masculine front to be considered a leader. I found myself resisting not only this style of leadership but also the stiff pinstriped suits paired with buttoned-up cotton blouses that were *de rigueur* at the time. I yearned for greater degrees of self-expression that felt more authentic to me.

As my career progressed, I encountered many hurdles—some extrinsic, including the realities of biases and stereotypes, as well as some intrinsic, like my own self-doubt and inner critic. Nevertheless, with determination and intentional, purpose-filled performance, I had many opportunities to lead with inclusivity and authenticity as hallmarks of my leadership brand, all centered on the support of my people and the people around me.

Over the years, I wished for more role models and diverse voices, especially those who were women, and I sought and found support from other women on parallel journeys. However, that support was often more ad hoc versus systemic, and there were times, especially in the first several decades of my professional journey, when it was especially challenging to find the help that I needed and the camaraderie that I craved. I vowed to become part of the solution as I advanced in my career. Thus, I committed myself to coaching, mentoring, and supporting hundreds and thousands of women through one-on-one relationships, one-to-many engagements, as well as through the creation of various women's programs, networks, and employee groups.

By the time I became an operating unit CEO in 2019, leading a business the size of a Fortune 100 company, I had built a robust career. I had also created a network of relationships with people who were as committed to catalyzing positive change as I was, especially in support of the advancement of women into more leadership roles, including the C-suite. It was in this role, as CEO of AT&T Business, that I first met Jennifer McCollum. I was immediately drawn to her and her organization, Linkage, with its mission to "Change the Face of Leadership." How powerfully said and how compellingly needed in a world that desires and requires more leaders who represent varying points of view, experiences, and perspectives, and who reflect the changing demographics of our communities, customers, and consumers (not to mention those of our investors, partners, and stakeholders)!

I quickly discovered that Jennifer and I share a pragmatic passion for the advancement of talented women across all industries and sectors.

I was honored when Linkage recognized me with their 2022 Legend in Leadership award during their Women in Leadership Institute. Jennifer and I sat down for a fireside chat covering a range of leadership topics in front of the 3,000 or so women present live and virtually. For me, this was a particularly powerful experience as I had recently retired from my role at AT&T and was in the early days of rewiring for the next chapters of my professional and personal impact. To be in the company of so many amazing women was absolutely energizing and inspiring.

And so, when Jennifer asked me to write the foreword for her new book, I gladly accepted. The reality is that we all want to advance in some way. Yes, many of us aspire to be the CEO of an organization and we know this with great certainty. But we don't quite know how to get there. Also, many of us are not sure what we're aspiring to—we only know that we can and want to have a greater impact. Perhaps we even long for our work to align with our life's purpose. But we don't quite know how to do that.

Regardless of where you've been or where you're going in your career and in life, no doubt you've run up against hurdles. And you've probably overcome some while others remained in your path. Maybe some even seem perpetual. It's likely that these hurdles have manifested themselves directly in front of you, around you, and even within you. Please know that you are not alone. The beauty of Jennifer's book is that it's based on the experiences of tens of thousands of women, and her guidance is applicable to every single one of us, no matter where we are on our own unique journey. The caring candor found in these pages is reflective of what happens—and can happen—in real life. I wish that I'd had the voices and experiences of these women at my side as I was progressing through my own career.

Your time is now. Our time is now. As women, it is our time to shine together. If each one of us develops and uses our voice, raising it with passion and purpose, there's no doubt that we can and will inspire generations of women leaders now and into the future. That's what this book is all about. Together, we're changing the face of leadership. After all, each one of us is the CEO of our life. Let's harness the power of our authenticity and determination. The world needs our voices and our leadership. May this moment become a movement, and may the words on these pages help you rise.

Anne Chow
Fortune's Most Powerful Women in Business 2020, 2021
Best-selling coauthor of *The Leader's Guide to Unconscious Bias*
Former CEO, AT&T Business

INTRODUCTION

Women, this is our moment to shine.

There has long been a shortage of women at the highest levels of leadership. Only 10 percent of Fortune 500 CEOs are women, and only 1 percent are women of color.[1] As we move down the leadership ranks, things improve a little but certainly aren't where they should be in an equitable world: in the United States, less than 30 percent of senior leadership positions and 40 percent of early manager positions are held by women.[2] And these numbers haven't changed much at all in the last decade. Globally, they are even worse.

This is not to say we haven't made some promising inroads. We have. But our progress has been excruciatingly slow, hampered at every turn by external bias, workplace inequities, microaggressions, sexual harassment, and even our own internalized fears and doubts. Despite the challenges, decade by decade we've continued to rise. I have a bird's-eye view of this reality from my position as CEO of a company dedicated to advancing women and other underrepresented groups into leadership roles. My own leadership journey hasn't been easy, though I wouldn't trade any of it. You'll get to hear more about my rise through corporate America, along with other women's stories that illustrate the power, potential, and promise of a future with gender equity in leadership.

So why write this book now? Because the COVID-19 pandemic changed everything. As the world, and especially the world of work, shifted so dramatically, I was simultaneously distressed to see so many women struggling and

excited about new possibilities. In the upcoming chapters, you'll learn that
the last few years have brought both unimaginable challenges and opportunities, specifically for women leaders.

Let's address the challenges first. When the pandemic hit, it was like
a tsunami for women leaders, destroying the fragile progress we'd been
making across the last few decades. The devastating result is that too many
women are downshifting in their roles or leaving the workforce altogether,
right when the world needs us most.

It's not hard to see why it's been so difficult. Life changed radically in
early 2020, and women took the hardest fall. Not only did our paid work
get tougher, so did our unpaid work. Trapped on endless video calls, many
of us desperately tried to help our bewildered kids navigate virtual school
while supporting our parents from afar. With the whole family sequestered
at home, housework demands skyrocketed. We had to negotiate physical
space and expectations with our partners while also being isolated from our
friends, extended family, and normal support networks. We were all scared,
overwhelmed, and exhausted. I was no exception.

Adjusting to these disruptions was daunting, but I fully acknowledge
that I had it easier than most. My kids were a bit older and more independent during the pandemic, and I had the means to pay for additional support, plus an involved husband who shares in household tasks. This is not
true for every woman. And for many, the pressure was too much. Women
either dropped out or were forced out of the workforce at an alarming rate.
Those who didn't—or couldn't—simply endured and muddled along the
best they could and found themselves at a breaking point. The world may
be rebounding now, but we still don't ultimately know how this will all
shake out for women in the longer term.

With pandemic-related struggles as a backdrop, it's not surprising that
35 percent of women in 2020 and 43 percent of women in 2021 reported
burnout.[3] In fact, a 2022 Deloitte Global survey of 5,000 women cited that
more than half intend to quit their jobs within the next two years, primarily due to burnout. The women surveyed felt more stressed than a year ago,

and one in three said they had taken time off due to their mental health, which nearly half reported to be "poor or very poor."[4]

Men, on the other hand, have not fared as badly. In 2021, women were experiencing two times the burnout rate of men and were three times more likely to be sidelined at work due to the increasing demands of home and family life.[5]

One of my own executive team members was so overwhelmed across 2020 by competing pressures from work and caring for a young child and an elderly mother that it exacerbated serious health issues. After taking a leave of absence (which I encouraged), she ended up leaving the corporate world altogether and starting a charcuterie and butcher business in a little seaside town. I supported her decision and want only the best for her. The fact that the Great Resignation—or its derivatives, "the Great Awakening" or "the Great Reimagining"—has inspired so many to reinvent themselves is a good thing. Everyone should pursue their dreams. Yet what's great for individuals like my colleague is *not* great for corporate America. Far from it.

Losing our women leaders and decimating our bench of the most promising next generation of executives would be a tragedy. And it's not just about the talent shortage; it's about losing access to women's unique gifts and abilities. Businesses need talented women, now more than ever. We need to do everything possible to engage, develop, and inspire them—and to advance them into leadership roles, all the way to the C-suite and board, if they so choose.

There is an abundance of research that proves the business case for women in leadership. Statistics show that companies with women represented at the top are 50 percent more likely to outperform their peers; they create better client retention, organic growth, and profit. Companies in the top quartile for gender diversity on executive teams are 25 percent more likely to outperform the competition.[6] And in the S&P 500, the 32 companies that have women as CEOs have significantly outperformed the companies run by men. Looking across the last decade, the difference in returns is 384 percent from female-led companies versus 261 percent from male-led companies.[7] A few notable companies with women CEOs to watch are General Motors, UPS, Citigroup, Walgreens, and CVS.

What's more, we're facing a massive shift in employee expectations as millennials and Gen Z become the dominant generations in the workforce. Women and men alike are insisting that companies embrace them as human beings, give them meaningful work, prioritize their well-being, and create a sense of inclusion and belonging that will allow them to fully contribute. In fact, more than 50 percent of millennial employees surveyed say they would leave their organization for a more inclusive one, while one third of the same demographic indicates they have already done so.[8] These trends have been unfolding for a while, but the COVID-19 years accelerated them, with a surge in the awareness of social injustice, the isolation of virtual work, and the systemic inequities that affect women and people of color the most. Now, as companies compete for scarce talent, they're being forced to reevaluate everything.

Part of responding to employees' new expectations is contemporizing workplace flexibility and benefits, but an even bigger part is making fundamental changes to the way we lead. Employee needs and wants *must* take center stage. Any vestigial "old school" management tendencies must be rooted out and replaced by leadership that inspires, engages, and transforms. This paradigm shift calls for the gifts that have been reinforced in women throughout their lives—gifts such as empathy, vulnerability, authenticity, and inclusion.

To respond to the evolving expectations of leadership, we must accelerate the advancement of women, and the solution is twofold: (1) organizations need to shift in fundamental ways that support and encourage women to move into leadership positions; and (2) individual women need to overcome the hurdles that keep us from advancing. *In Her Own Voice* is written to help us achieve both goals.

Most of the book presents insights developed by my organization, Linkage. For more than three decades, we've committed ourselves to "Changing the Face of Leadership" by advancing women and accelerating inclusion in leaders and organizations. We've discovered that women leaders perform better, stay at their companies longer, and advance in their careers when organizations properly address four critical dimensions:

* **Culture:** Do we as women feel valued and respected in our organization? Do we feel like our uniqueness is honored and that we belong?
* **People Systems & Processes:** Do we have equal opportunities in people systems like the hiring process, access to stretch assignments, or promotions and sponsorship?
* **Executive Action:** Are executives *really* committed to inclusivity and taking action to support and sponsor women (or do they just pay lip service to this goal)?
* **Leadership Development:** Do we have access to and take advantage of effective development for women? This is about our own development as a leader. We ultimately have the most control over our own thoughts and actions, which is why I've made it the primary focus of this book.

We call this the *Strategic Framework to Advance Women Leaders,* and we will discuss it in more detail in the book's final chapters.

So why wait until later to explore what companies can do to help women advance when it is so obviously and deeply important? Our belief at Linkage is that there is great power in helping women at the individual level to understand and overcome what's standing in our own way. Through our 25 years of women's leadership research, assessment, development, and coaching, Linkage has uncovered what we call the *hurdles* to women's advancement.

These hurdles—*The Inner Critic, Internal Bias, Clarity, Proving Your Value, Recognized Confidence, Branding & Presence, Making the Ask,* and *Networking*—will be thoroughly explored in the upcoming chapters, as well as the strategies for overcoming them.

Throughout the book, I use the metaphor of a journey. Journeys are, of course, undertaken by individuals. And while the lioness's share of the work is on women, there is much our companies need to do to support us on that journey. When they do, we all win.

We are continuously inspired by the thousands of women leaders who report they are transformed when they focus on their own development. They attend our immersive Women in Leadership Institute™, they work through their Advancing Women Leaders 360° assessment with a coach, or they join their peers in a development program designed to help women overcome the hurdles. Specifically, they cite an increase in confidence, compensation, recognition for their contributions, and, my favorite, their understanding of their unique strengths and talents as a leader.

Organizations benefit, too. Our data shows that these same women who have received investment in their development are more engaged, have more personal satisfaction with their work, are more likely to stay with their company, and lead teams that are outperforming the company average.

So, given the obvious benefits to both individual women and their organizations, how *are* companies doing in their efforts to advance women? Well, it's complicated.

Linkage has tracked women's perceptions of their organizations since 2016, and we've aggregated data on more than 16,000 women across industries and companies globally. We measure the four dimensions in our Strategic Framework model described above, as well as Engagement, Commitment, Values Fit, and Net Promoter Score ("Would you recommend this company as a great place for women to work?"). All these metrics give us leading indicators about what's happening year to year with women in terms of how they feel about their organization.

As we emerge from these pandemic years, the data is revealing the toll these challenging times have had on women, and it's alarming. In 2021, for the first time since we'd been tracking this data, every single leading indicator declined, and Net Promoter Scores plummeted.[9] This shed important light on exactly why women were threatening to change jobs, downshift in their careers, or leave the workforce. By 2022, that trend had been confirmed with what McKinsey called "the Great Breakup," which saw 10.5

percent of women changing jobs versus 9 percent of men.[10] Most concerning, the study showed that for every woman director promoted to vice president, two women directors left. These are the very women in the pipeline to become vice presidents and executives. We are at the breaking point.

Yet there's also plenty of good news. In mid-2020, Goldman Sachs declared it would not take a company public in the United States or Europe unless there was at least one diverse board candidate, with a focus on women. In June 2021, Business Roundtable, led by Chair and CEO of General Motors Mary Barra, launched an initiative to promote increased transparency on corporate diversity by companies voluntarily disclosing their diversity metrics. There is a dramatic increase in the number of women and people of color on corporate boards,[11] and we could see gender equity there first. And I witness many Linkage clients working tirelessly, year after year, to build cultures where women leaders can excel.

I certainly feel encouraged by these steps in the right direction, yet I feel a sense of urgency because the journey toward women's advancement in leadership is taking too much time with too little progress. The World Economic Forum had predicted prior to COVID-19 that it would take 100 years to close the gender equality gap, a timeline that has now been extended by 36 more years because of the pandemic impact.[12] I believe we can—and must—do all we can to shorten that time frame in our lifetime.

We need more women in more leadership roles, from the production floor to the highest corner offices on Wall Street. The companies that understand this and act to develop women leaders will set themselves up to thrive in a world that has been shaken to its foundation. The women leaders who rise to the occasion and set out on the journey will have the great privilege of shaping a stronger, more inclusive, more productive world for all.

Women, this is our moment. Let's move forward together.

PART ONE

Understanding the Hurdles to Women's Advancement

1

External Bias and Its Impact on the Advancement of Women

In many ways, the journey to overcoming hurdles is a deeply personal one, and one that looks different for each woman. But before we can talk about *you*—the individual woman who wants to grow, advance, and help others be all they can be—we must acknowledge the reality of the environment around us. No woman is an island. We must contend with the implied "rules" and expectations of the society in which we live and lead.

Our society doesn't always view women the way we might wish to be viewed. Specifically, it doesn't view us the way it views men; it has different expectations for us based on well-documented biases we'll cover in this book. At times, this reality isn't a problem. But many other times, like when we are trying to reach higher levels of leadership, external bias is incredibly frustrating and limiting.

In short, gender bias occurs when people show favoritism toward one gender over another. Whether this behavior is conscious or unconscious, the result is that men and women are treated differently. Today, gender bias generally refers to the preferential treatment men—specifically white heterosexual men—receive. This does not make men the bad guys. It's a reality resulting from a long history of certain societal expectations and experiences that we have all internalized.

Bias is hardwired into our brains to help us make sense of the world quickly. It helps us cope with complexity, reduce danger, and make decisions. The challenge becomes when biases transform into prejudice, differential treatment, and inequality based on specific demographics. A clear example of bias against women is inequitable treatment when it comes to pay. The pay gap between men and women starts as early as 16, and the lifetime loss of earnings of women over 40 compared to men overall is $406,280, and it's even worse for Black women at $964,400 and Latinas at $1,163,920.[1] Additional biases include inequitable access to mentors and sponsors, promotion potential, and selection for senior roles. There is evidence, however, that awareness of these external biases has shifted significantly over the last five years.

The #MeToo movement[2] in 2017 brought gender bias to the forefront, shedding light on the sexual abuse and harassment women have historically faced in the workforce. While the movement began in 2006 when activist Tarana Burke coined the term, it received mainstream recognition following the severe sexual assault allegations against Harvey Weinstein. The movement surfaced awareness of inappropriate behavior in the workplace, from assault to sexual harassment to the microaggressions often born of unconscious bias that undermine women's progress and harm our well-being.

While #MeToo instigated a wake-up call about gender inequity, the goal of the movement was not to accelerate the advancement of women in leadership. What *did* move bias awareness to action, however, was COVID-19 and its aftermath. The pandemic years have illuminated the disproportionate burden women face with their "second shift" of home, child, and elder care and the newer "third shift" that women also fulfill with additional employee care and office "housework." McKinsey's research in 2021 surfaced that women, and mothers in particular, are three times more likely than fathers to be responsible for most of the housework and caregiving, which peaked at an additional three hours per day during the pandemic.[3]

Beyond the division of labor, men and women experience the world in vastly different ways, largely based on how over centuries women have internalized the gender biases we face. Let me illustrate using a story about something as seemingly simple as negotiating effectively for what you want.

In November 2021, I had the privilege of introducing Magic Johnson as a keynote speaker at our 22nd annual Linkage Women in Leadership Institute™. Magic is an incredible advocate for women, particularly women of color, which is why we invited him to speak at our conference. Magic was inspiring and fearless; it seemed nothing ever stood in his way, even after reinventing himself many times from NBA superstar sidelined by HIV to one of the most successful business moguls in the world.

He was addressing 2,600 women in our live and virtual audience on the topic of being bold as a leader, reinforcing the need for women to *make the ask* for what they want—and expect to get it. Magic was radiating charm and brimming with confidence as he told his truly amazing story. I was monitoring audience questions as they poured in electronically on an iPad, where I tried to prioritize them. Mostly, based on the questions, it was clear these women were perplexed by the differences they saw between their own realities and how Magic saw the world. I peppered him with the audience questions:

> *Did you ever want something but were too afraid to ask?* "No," Magic answered.
>
> *Did you ever ask for something and not get it?* "Not really," he answered again.
>
> *Did you ever walk away if you were denied?* "No again," he laughed.

He was inspiring and energizing, but ultimately, the audience of women, who experience fear regularly when making critically important asks—around career progression, pay, flexibility, or resources—had trouble relating to his experience. So I switched tactics and reframed the questions to be more relevant to him personally:

> *How do you advise the women leaders who work for you to be bold and ask for what they want?*
> *What do you tell your daughter about being bold?*

It was clear from his reaction to the second line of questioning that he had never considered a gender lens to his natural penchant for going after whatever he wanted—and getting it. His persona shifted, and his self-assurance seemed to falter for a moment. My perception was that he was grappling for answers to the questions—and it seemed his advice for women boiled down to "Just do what I do!"

I was now getting a bit desperate for the women to connect to his story, so I finally looked at the audience, shrugged my shoulders, and smiled as if to say, "Do you get it? Magic is demonstrating to us what bold looks like— but we simply can't see ourselves in his examples."

While Magic's words were entertaining and engaging, most of the women in the audience couldn't relate to his approach, for good reason. Typically, the path to leadership is very different for us. We face challenges that men rarely have to consider, based foundationally on externalized bias. Additionally, we have carried the burden of unreasonable societal expectations of acting like a male leader while still fulfilling all the obligations of a caretaker, which have historically rested on the shoulders of women.

EXTERNAL BIAS IMPACTS US ALL

Every woman I know has stories about how she has encountered externalized bias throughout her career. Social norms have evolved significantly across the last three decades, and the overt harassment many women experienced is—thankfully—now widely publicized and scorned.

For me, I didn't have role models or mentors in the corporate world when I started my internships and first several jobs. When working in the 1990s, I constantly dodged aggressive behavior by men in positions of power and influence and observed other women doing the same. I just assumed that was how the corporate world worked and that if I could figure out how to play the game without crossing any lines, I would progress in my career. It never occurred to me in my first decade of corporate work that the leadership majority—all white men—was playing by a completely different set of rules.

In my coveted internship during graduate school, I had the opportunity to work for a corporate sponsor of the 1992 Olympic Games in Barcelona. It was thrilling, and alongside my paid work as an assistant and translator, I could gain access to the most senior leaders in the company to complete interviews for my master's thesis. My boss was a woman, but her peer—we'll call him Matt—was a gregarious man who had the network I needed to complete my critical assignment that summer. He promised to broker the introductions for me. It soon became clear that the introductions came with a cost.

At an outdoor dinner with a high-ranking executive and his wife, Matt proceeded to grab my legs under the table, while I did my best to carry on a professional conversation about my research. I nervously moved his hands away throughout the evening, which only encouraged him to keep trying. I was now stuck. I needed his access and support to complete my degree but feared his unwanted advances were a prerequisite to achieving my goal. It didn't even cross my mind to tell anyone because I assumed this was just the price of entry into the business world. When Matt's girlfriend—and subsequent fiancée—arrived for the end of the event, Matt finally shifted his attention elsewhere, and I finished my master's thesis with the highest distinction.

This is one of many, many stories I could tell, and I know most women have similar ones or worse. I share mine because so often women hide theirs, either due to shame or fear. Why didn't I tell my boss what was happening and seek her counsel? Might I have found a colleague who had navigated similar experiences? Instead, I kept all those stories secret, believing I had enough good sense to strike the right balance between accepting the behavior while preventing any serious transgression. It was a dangerous game.

It is only now in retrospect, 30 years later, that I clearly see those situations for what they were—overt sexual harassment. I'm grateful that millennial and Gen Z women leaders have many more role models than I did, with brave victims speaking out and perpetrators facing consequences. I talk openly now with my own daughter and other rising leaders I mentor to ensure we create a healthier work environment where everyone feels safe and comfortable sharing their experiences. We have moved squarely in the right direction with confronting harassment in the workplace, but we need to continue to share these stories to foster greater awareness and understanding.

The other area where we're making good progress, albeit slowly, is equity in our talent systems. A few years after my internship, I secured a full-time marketing communications role at the same company that allowed me to travel around the world and experience other work cultures. What I found was that cultural norms in many countries had even more deeply embedded biases against women as leaders and decision makers. While my male peers in these countries were welcoming and polite, they simply did not recognize me as having any real authority. When I was up for a promotion that would relocate me to Costa Rica, it was offered to a man who many told me later was less qualified.

Back in the United States, things weren't much better. Three years into my tenure, I was promoted and shifted into the role of corporate liaison for public affairs and communications, working directly with all the local field offices in Europe. I was younger than my peers in our corporate headquarters, and even though we had the same role, I learned over time that I was paid significantly less. I rationalized it as having less tenure in my position and vowed silently to put my head down and work harder than anyone else, with the confidence that my superiors would notice and give me additional compensation as I progressed. As a year or two passed, however, my raises and bonuses never caught up with my peers' compensation.

I also became resentful of the office space dilemma. At the time, having an exterior office was a status symbol. All my peers had beautiful offices with large windows overlooking downtown, but as the last one promoted into the role, there were no additional windowed offices available. I was stuck in a drab interior office, but I again chalked it up to tenure. I assumed my time would come.

And then it did. When the Latin America liaison left his role, my boss decided to hire the local public relations director from Spain. Rafael, a fabulous professional and colleague whom I'd worked with regularly, planned his move from Spain to our US corporate headquarters, while I plotted my own move to the open office with a window. My manager, Rob, had been at the company for decades. He was a brilliant professional and supportive boss. I walked into his office to request the office that I had earned, but he told me it had been earmarked for Rafael.

I didn't understand. I knew it wasn't fair, but instead of assuming this was an example of bias, I assumed I hadn't earned it.

I blurted out, "What am I doing wrong?"

Rob looked at me, confused.

"I've been in my role for more than a year now, and I'm the only one without a window office," I continued. "Rafael is new to the role, but he's moving straight into the office that I deserve. So, I must be doing something wrong, or you would have given it to me."

And then I burst into tears.

I'm not sure if it was the fact that I brought the inequity to his attention or that I became emotional about the injustice of it all, but Rob wasted no time in giving me the office. He apologized and thanked me for bringing it to his awareness. Unconscious bias had suddenly been made visible.

At the time, I was embarrassed that I broke down in his office. However, similar episodes have happened a handful of times in my decades of business, whether I'm the one shedding tears or it's one of my female colleagues or direct reports. I have come to welcome the entire spectrum of emotion, realizing that bringing our full authenticity into the workplace is part of what will free women to leverage our natural gifts and step into our true power as leaders. The idea that emotion is weakness is yet another bias to break down. Perhaps rather than exhorting women to try to squelch theirs, we should encourage men to express emotion more often—or at least become more comfortable and accepting when their colleagues do.

One of the most difficult manifestations of externalized bias is the double bind for women. It's a constant tightrope we walk. We must balance the irreconcilable demands of meeting societal expectations for women—demonstrating female characteristics, like being *compassionate, warm, communicative*, and *collaborative*—with the expectations for leaders, which are dominated by male characteristics of being *forceful, assertive, dominant*, and *competitive*. The dilemma is that when women display the male characteristics of "taking charge," they are seen as competent but aren't liked. Conversely, when we display the female characteristics of "taking care," we are viewed as less competent.

Catalyst, a global nonprofit with a mission to help build workplaces that work for women, captures this dilemma well[4] (see image on page 19).

Ideally, men and women alike would incorporate both styles of leadership—taking charge and taking care—into the evolving expectations of what the most effective leaders do. However, the current external bias forces only women to be seen as either taking charge *or* taking care rather than placing the same expectation on men to embrace both.

The double bind is exhausting for women. This externalized bias of strong leadership qualities being perceived as "male" holds women to a higher standard than it does men. It requires us to spend much more time

GENDER STEREOTYPES CREATE A NO-WIN SITUATION FOR WOMEN LEADERS

STEREOTYPE	DOUBLE BIND

Men Take Charge
- Strong
- Decisive
- Assertive

When women **take charge,** they are viewed as competent leaders—but disliked.

Women Take Care
- Nurturing
- Emotional
- Communicative

When women **take care,** they are liked—but viewed as less competent leaders.

RESULT   Women leaders are seen as competent or likeable, but rarely both.

© Catalyst Inc. 2018. Use pursuant to license.

at work proving ourselves as competent while hiding or downplaying the natural strengths we bring to leadership to live up to the male-dominated stereotypes of leadership.

It was decades after I began my career that I realized how this external bias had trapped me in every leadership role. Today, when I hear anyone call a woman leader too "aggressive" or "ambitious," I take a deep breath and tell my best double-bind story.

The Double Bind in Real Life: The Cupcake with a Razor Blade

It was 1996, and I was destined to prove myself as a competent manager in a dream job I had just secured as a public relations manager at the Coca-Cola Company. My first assignment was managing the news media and branding for Coca-Cola's title sponsorship of the Olympic Torch Relay. The company had aligned its brand to the Olympic flame for decades, but this Olympic Games was special, as it was being hosted in Atlanta, home of the Coca-Cola headquarters.

We had a talented team of more than 100 people working to ensure the company received positive recognition for the Olympic flame's migration from Athens to Atlanta. It was a celebratory caravan that would span 87 days, 42 states, and 15,000 miles and honor 10,000 carefully selected torch-bearers, a group comprising local community heroes.

There is always natural tension between an Olympic Organizing Committee and the sponsors who are critical to helping fund and acti-vate the Games. The Olympic Rings are held as pure and sacred, and the brand is protected fiercely by the International Olympic Committee and the local Olympic organizers. However, the sponsors need to benefit from their significant investments in the form of public awareness, posi-tive association, and, ultimately, loyalty to and purchase of their products. I was determined to win the brand battle for Coca-Cola as we shared the Olympic flame with the Unites States across the days, weeks, and months leading up to the Opening Ceremonies. I was focused, ambitious, and competitive in my quest to prove myself a worthy professional in this very visible role.

David was my counterpart on the Atlanta Olympic Committee, and I needed to cooperate and collaborate with him to succeed, but I also needed to meet the clear objectives of my assignment. He quickly became my rival, trying to prevent our media blitz and block our team from access to the very reporters we needed to engage. Ultimately, we lost some battles but won the overall war. In the process, I knew I was disliked by the Olympic Committee's communications team, but in my relentless pursuit of victory and accolades from my own bosses, I accepted my role as "villain" and persisted.

Our weary team was greeted by wildly cheering colleagues at the Coca-Cola headquarters as the caravan with the Olympic flame made a final stop before the Opening Ceremonies that evening. My boss, a brilliant Brit named Brendan Harris, bounded up to me at the finale of our three-month odyssey to congratulate me on a job well done. He had a huge grin on his face and said, "You'll never believe what David just called you—it's hilarious." I looked at Brendan in anticipation as he casually dropped a mental image I still can't erase more than 25 years later. "He said, 'Jennifer is like a cupcake with a razor blade inside.'"

Brendan interpreted this comment as a point of pride, a description of a deceptively soft, sweet, lovely outer package with a sharp, deadly, fierce weapon concealed inside. And while I wasn't sure it was an insult, it certainly didn't strike me as a compliment. I was first confused, and later devastated.

I now see this analogy for what it is: a perfect example of the double bind that women have faced since entering the professional ranks, toggling between all the expectations of the masculine stereotype of the ideal leader (the razor blade) alongside the feminine stereotypes of the ideal woman (the cupcake). A man would never be described that way.

It is only in retrospect that I acknowledge the real challenge we need to overcome—the perception that a woman can only be either the cupcake *or* the razor blade, when in fact we need the entire spectrum of gender operating as both "taking charge" and "taking care." The feminine force and characteristics should not be perceived as purely fluffy and soft; nor should masculine energy be seen as a force that purely slashes and destroys. We are all complex and multifaceted, with different strengths, and we are all higher manifestations than the stereotypes we're often reduced to. It is in honoring and integrating strengths across gender roles that all leaders will become more effective.

THE TRIPLE BIND

The double bind gets worse for women of color. Besides fulfilling the expectations of a leader and a woman, they must absorb the additional cultural expectations that come with race. In our Linkage research that layers race on top of gender using 360° feedback data, we see real and measurable behavioral differences between women leaders of different racial or ethnic identities.

Simply put, we can't treat all women as one homogeneous group.

The bigger challenge, however, is the *perceptual* differences, resulting in increased bias that women from underrepresented racial and ethnic groups experience. That happens when there is consistent disagreement between the women's self-ratings and other raters. For example, other raters in our study did not acknowledge the strengths that Black women leaders see in themselves, such as their ability to control and filter emotions in a constructive manner or to be open-minded or unlimited in thinking about their own capability and potential to achieve. The same was true for Latina women leaders, where raters did not acknowledge the strengths Latina women believe they have, such as their ability to have an impact on important decisions made in the organization or their ability to stimulate strong commitment to collective efforts through praise and recognition of individual contributors.

Raters also had inaccurate stereotype biases, assigning weakness in areas that were not true. For example, raters made unsupported assumptions that Black or multiracial women leaders are less likely to clearly define and communicate a strategic direction. Also, raters had some positivity bias toward Asian/South Asian women leaders—who were rated more highly by others than by themselves—with inaccurate assumptions around their ability to skillfully complement formal authority with effective personal influence or demonstrate openness and appreciation of others' viewpoints. Similarly, white women leaders had raters inaccurately assume their strength in clearly defining and communicating strategic direction, speaking assertively, being willing to promote themselves and their ideas, and asking for what they want and need.

The point of all of this is that white women leaders often have a distinct advantage over other racial/ethnic groups when it comes to positivity bias, as white women leaders are assessed more favorably by others than how they assess themselves.

The Triple Bind in Real Life: The Vice President Live on National Television

The triple bind was on full display during the 2020 vice presidential debate between Kamala Harris and Mike Pence. The debate may be best remembered by the fly that landed on Pence's head for two minutes, distracting the viewers away from the content of the candidates. But I will always remember Harris, who is biracial and identifies as Black, being interrupted repeatedly by her very assertive opponent. She seemed to force a smile, trying her best to display the warmth, patience, and kindness expected of a woman, all the while working to push her way into the conversation so she could land her points succinctly and credibly.

The fact that she is a biracial woman only added to the challenge, as Black women particularly are often accused of being aggressive and not keeping their emotions in check. This Harris trifecta—leader, woman, Black—was mesmerizing to watch, and I moved my attention away from the fly to Harris's body language and words.

"Mr. Vice President, I'm speaking. I'm speaking." She said it again and again, through clenched teeth and a fixed smile. "If you don't mind letting me finish, we can then have a conversation, okay?"

Indeed, NBCNews.com reported that Pence interrupted Harris 16 times to her 9 interruptions and made 93 "attacks" to her 84 "attacks."[5] While we won't ever know Pence's awareness or motivation behind the overweighted interruptions, it is something that most businesswomen have painfully witnessed or experienced many times over.

As I witnessed the tension of the ongoing debate and noted and watched the stilted and measured Harris, I could feel the bind. If she raised her voice instead of being gracious, she could be accused of being too aggressive—not an acceptable stereotype for a woman. If she became angry, she could be criticized for not controlling her emotions, falling into the stereotype of the "angry Black woman." If she stayed silent, she wouldn't get her point across or be seen as a credible or competent leader. Whether this was consciously playing out in her experience or not, I could see the dilemma she was in—and that Pence was not. Men do not even have to consider these types of debilitating stereotypes.

To be clear, Harris had good reason for concern. Even as she was being vetted as a qualified candidate for the vice president of the United States in mid-2020, CNBC reported that "Some argue that she's too ambitious and that she will be solely focused on eventually becoming president."[6]

The truth is women have historically been appreciated and recognized in the supportive role they play in lifting the leadership majority. Seeing women—especially women of color—leading from the front, whether in politics or business, can be uncomfortable for many, especially those who are currently in positions of power. It's time for all of us to embrace that discomfort by honoring, supporting, and celebrating all women who are stepping into their own ambition and leadership. We need to normalize this as a human right: to contribute all we have to offer and be rewarded and recognized for it.

Thankfully, there are encouraging signs that attitudes toward assertive women are changing. In fact, a 2020 *Forbes* article I contributed to points out that then-candidate Joe Biden treated Harris with respect, even when her assertiveness meant questioning him on his past race-related policies. The author points out that by choosing her as a running mate he "demonstrates he wants a partner in governance, one who is not afraid to speak truth to power."[7]

IN THE FACE OF BIAS, WHAT CAN
WE ACTUALLY CONTROL?

As much as we awaken ourselves and others to external bias, we can't control it. We can't make the double and triple binds go away, at least not quickly enough to create gender equity in the next century. Therefore, the focus of this book is to help women with what we *can* control in terms of developing the awareness, understanding, and skills to scale the hurdles that we have internalized based on the real bias we face externally. While these hurdles are hard to identify and overcome, our purpose is to guide women in soaring over them to accelerate their own advancement, while simultaneously working with organizations to eradicate centuries of bias that have prevented these very women from achieving equal pay, position, and power in the workplace.

2

The Hurdles to Women's Advancement: A Brief Overview

We've just reviewed the societal biases that, collectively, hold so many women back. Now we're going to get more specific about some individual challenges many of us have internalized as a result. For more than 25 years, Linkage has been tracking the unique challenges women face on the path toward holding more senior levels of leadership. We call them hurdles, and while men can certainly face them as well, they are higher and harder to overcome for women.

The first big, overarching hurdle to advancement is the Inner Critic. It amplifies all the other hurdles:

* Internal Bias
* Clarity
* Proving Your Value
* Recognized Confidence

* Branding & Presence
* Making the Ask
* Networking

27

We'll discuss each hurdle in a bit more detail momentarily; then, as we go through the book, we'll devote an entire chapter to each one.

Linkage discovered the hurdles as they emerged in our work through assessments, coaching, and developing women with some of the world's leading companies, including Constellation Brands, Disney, Lenovo, and Oracle. We first published the hurdles in Linkage's 2018 book, *Mastering Your Inner Critic and 7 Other High Hurdles to Advancement* by Susan MacKenty Brady, a former Linkage executive and founder of Linkage's Women in Leadership Institute™. Going further, *In Her Own Voice* reflects what we have learned in the last many years as the working environment has changed so significantly—especially for women—with both the challenge and opportunity that came with more flexible, virtual, and remote work during the COVID-19 pandemic and beyond.

In our leadership assessments of more than 120,000 women and their raters gathered from 2016 to 2022, we have been tracking and measuring

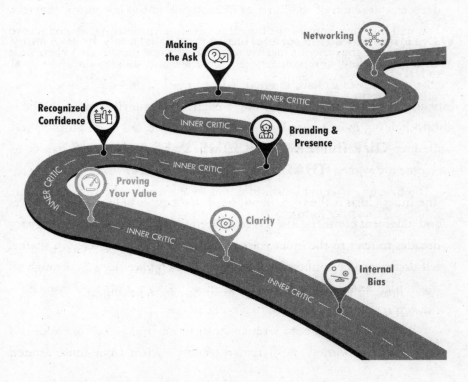

women's progress on these hurdles, as reported by the women themselves along with the perception of each woman's manager, direct reports, and peers. The hurdles have emerged consistently and reliably, and we have proven we can help women overcome them.

While each of us individually has natural strengths and challenges related to each hurdle, the three that women most frequently struggle with are Proving Your Value, Clarity, and Making the Ask. The hurdles that score the "strongest," meaning we have made good progress in overcoming them, are Branding & Presence and Networking. This could be because these topics have been a primary focus in women's leadership development since the industry first emerged more formally in the 1990s. The very encouraging news is that as we track women's progress year over year, we are making great strides; our data shows that women themselves believe they are improving, and their rater groups agree.

We'll take a quick look at each of the hurdles before we move into deeper exploration of the nuances of each one in the upcoming chapters. You will find that none of the hurdles exists in a vacuum—they connect to and reinforce the others. Once we learn to clear one hurdle, the others start to feel easier.

Let's begin.

OUR INNER CRITIC: THE "MEGA HURDLE" THAT NEVER GOES AWAY

The Inner Critic is the voice in our head that creates judgment of ourselves and judgment of others. The term has been used by popular psychology for decades to refer to the inner voice that attacks us, leaving us with shame, self-doubt, or low confidence. The Inner Critic weaves its way through all the hurdles and, at times, amplifies them to make our progress more difficult or prevents us from taking action at all.

While we are not born with an Inner Critic, it develops in childhood as we hear or witness harsh remarks and criticism from those around us—parents, peers, teachers, etc. It can also stem from hearing adults speak harshly about themselves. Over time, this repeated exposure changes the wiring in our brain, becomes internalized, and creates a filter through which we see the world as adults.

I don't think I need to tell you how harmful the Inner Critic can be. Obviously, it can generate enough fear and uncertainty to stop us from acting. It can also drive us to criticize others, which is detrimental to building the positive relationships we need to not only advance in our careers but also lead in a way that encourages growth in those around us. But if we can get better and faster at recognizing our Inner Critic, we can learn to coach it, moderate the harshness it leads us to express, and reduce its negative impact on ourselves and others. In doing so, the Inner Critic becomes a gift that can help us overcome the other hurdles. It helps us build the awareness required to change and improve as a leader.

Here's an illustration: A few of my colleagues at Linkage informed me upon my arrival in 2018 that they were surprised a woman had actually been chosen as CEO for the first time, given the organization's 30-year history of male CEOs. The truth is, I was surprised, too—not that I had earned the job but that I had even put myself in the running.

When a headhunter approached me about the CEO role, my Inner Critic took over the thoughts in my head. It sounded like this:

* I'm not ready for the top job; I need to be a #2 first so I can be properly groomed.
* I've never managed the P&L from top to bottom before—there is too much I don't know.
* My oldest kids are heading into high school, and they need me; I won't be available for them during their teen years.
* And therefore . . . someone else would be better.

Blah, blah, blah. You aren't ready, you aren't qualified, you won't get it anyway. My Inner Critic was relentless. If Simon, Christoffer, and Andrew—trusted men in my peer and advisory network—hadn't intervened and stopped me in my swirl, I don't think I would have entered the CEO game at all. "If not now, when?" they asked. "You are as ready now as you will ever be." They said this quickly and without thinking, as if it were a conclusion they had drawn long ago. But it was an awakening for me.

This is the perfect example of why, as we will explore later in this book, we need to enlist men as allies, mentors, and sponsors in advancing women leaders. Think about the raw confidence Magic Johnson exhibited. Men can often demonstrate to us women how to tap into that sense of self-assurance our Inner Critic seems determined to squelch.

The Inner Critic is always present. It is simply part of who we are. However, with curiosity, it can be harnessed and calmed, and we'll discuss how in the next chapter. For now, let's jump into the seven other hurdles women uniquely face.

HURDLE 1: INTERNAL BIAS

What deeply held beliefs do you hold about yourself that no longer serve you? Here we are not addressing the individual beliefs or biases of others, which are external and may lead those in positions of power to network, hire, develop, or promote people like themselves. Nor are we talking about organizational biases in talent systems, like performance management processes or compensation policies. For example, a study from MIT Sloan associate professor Danielle Li found that "female employees are less likely to be promoted than their male counterparts, despite outperforming them and being less likely to quit."[1] She uncovered that even though women rank higher in objective *performance* scores, men rank higher in subjective *potential* scores, and potential ratings are predictive of promotions.[2] That's external bias, and that is out of our control.

The biases we are talking about here are your own. While influenced by external bias, internal biases are your assumptions and beliefs that might either propel you forward or hold you back. Here are some of my own internal biases I've surfaced and tried to change across the course of my career:

1. Things are done better when I do them myself.
2. I can't be an engaged, involved mom if I have a big job.
3. I need to have CEO experience before I can be a CEO.

It's not hard to see that these are limiting beliefs. Because we act (or, rather, don't act) on them, they shape the trajectory of our lives. The good news is that, often, these limiting beliefs don't hold up under scrutiny. They may be rooted in stories we've told ourselves for years, maybe even a lifetime. If we can surface them, we can determine whether these stories hold true.

Just like with the Inner Critic, curiosity helps deepen your understanding of your internal bias. You can pause and ask yourself, "Is this a core belief? Can I revisit it? What happens if I overwrite it with a new story that serves me better?" In my case, the CEO job was a *different* big job, but I'd just spent a decade in other big jobs: for instance, running business units in publicly traded companies. Was I able to (mostly) be the type of mom I wanted to be while in those roles? The answer was yes . . . so why would the CEO job change that?

Biases need to be checked continuously, as they will surface again and again until you give them less power. On my son Hunter's 14th birthday, I was on a train to New York City while his father took him to Benihana for his traditional birthday dinner. Knowing I would miss it consumed me with guilt. Leading up to his big day, I reminded myself again and again: "I can't be the kind of mom I want to be with this job." So, I overcompensated: I got up early to make him breakfast and open presents, I drove him to school before jumping on the train, I texted and called him a few times throughout the day, and I posted birthday wishes on Snapchat and Instagram. By that evening, when I called him at Benihana, he was a little exasperated and said, "Mom, I'm good. You've wished me a happy birthday six times today! You can stop now." Clearly, my own bias wasn't in line with my son's perception or expectations.

HURDLE 2: CLARITY

How do we create intention about our future and professional advancement? Do you know the answer when someone asks, "What do you want for the next chapter in your career?" Many women do not. Gaining clarity has been harder in these last few years because of the pressure to manage so many additional priorities in the shifting swirl of COVID-19 and virtual work, with childcare, house care, and employee care all competing for focus alongside our "day jobs." It's a core reason women lost a net 5.4 million more jobs than men did during the pandemic.[3] While more women than men worked in sectors where jobs were eliminated—like hospitality, tourism, and retail—even more left the workforce because they simply didn't have the resources, the capacity, or the will to carry on in the status quo under such impossible circumstances.

Interestingly, we know now from 2022 research by Harvard economics professor Claudia Goldin that college-educated mothers did not leave the workforce at greater numbers than men, largely because they worked in roles that could be done remotely. However, she writes that women "have been stressed, frustrated, and anxious because they did *not* leave their jobs" and took on much more of the caregiving work at the same time—at home and at work.[4]

As we began to emerge out of the pandemic storm across 2021, these very COVID-19 complications spurred what is now called the "Great Resignation" and the "Great Breakup." Women finally started to get clarity on the kind of work we wanted to do, the flexibility and control we wanted over our work schedule, and the culture and office environment that would best support us.

The circumstances were so intense and extraordinary that they really forced clarity, like in the case of my executive team member who left the corporate world to pursue a lifelong dream. But we shouldn't wait for a crisis to focus on what we most want with our career and to share it with others. As we'll discuss in chapter five, it takes intention, dedicated time, and practice to "do the work" to find clarity. Once we *do* achieve it, again and again throughout our career, all the other hurdles become exponentially easier. And as a bonus, the act of discovering and pursuing what you want is immensely energizing!

HURDLE 3: PROVING YOUR VALUE

How can we stop doing so much? The tendency for many of us to work harder and harder stems from the internal bias that rings true for so many women: *If it's going to get done right, I have to do it myself.* The result is something we call "over-rowing the boat." We keep grinding away with the assumption that it will pay off in the future. But most of the time, we're actually rowing ourselves straight into complete overwhelm.

As we've discussed, at the height of COVID-19, women daily, on average, were putting in *well over* their standard three additional hours of "the second shift." These post-workday hours got even harder as we struggled to manage family lives and school schedules that had been turned upside down. Meanwhile, we were learning a new way of working while also putting in extra effort to help our coworkers. It's no wonder we became increasingly burned out.

As we rise in organizations, we are forced to realize that we can't keep doing it ourselves and hoping people will notice. They probably won't. Instead, we can release any perfectionism and start to rely more on others. That means inspiring them to work toward an aspirational goal, delegating some of the load, and asking for help. We can also set better boundaries by being much more intentional about when, why, and how we say no. Clarity helps us with all of this.

I have had a very fulfilling career. While it's not over, if I could go back 30 years and give my younger self a few words of advice as I moved up in management ranks, it would be this: "Take your foot off the gas a bit. You don't have to do it all to prove yourself at home, at work, and in the community. Choose the work that aligns with your passion and strength. And don't assume that hard work will be noticed and rewarded—ensure that you are seen in your accomplishments."

In the hit musical *Hamilton*, Aaron Burr advises Alexander to "talk less; smile more." Along these lines, I would try to "do less; engage more"—with peers, direct reports, and senior leaders.

HURDLE 4: RECOGNIZED CONFIDENCE

Do others see your accomplishments because you are able to both demonstrate your competence and ensure others recognize it, too? Women need to take more action to exhibit confidence and share our successes with key people. Men actually do this very well. A Hewlett-Packard internal study showed that men applied for new roles when they met only 60 percent of the job criteria, while women didn't apply until they met 100 percent. In other words, "men are confident about their ability at 60%, but women don't feel confident until they've checked off each item on the list,"[5] a phenomenon we'll explore more in the next chapter.

It's no secret that women do struggle more with confidence, a struggle that starts well before women hit the workforce. In their book *The Confidence Code*, Katty Kay and Claire Shipman write about their research with polling firm YPulse that found girls' confidence levels plunge by 30 percent between the ages of 8–14. According to a *Time* article the two penned along with JillEllyn Riley, "Boys do experience some bumps in confidence entering their teens. But at 14, when girls are hitting their low, boys' confidence is still 27% higher. And the effects are long-lasting. For most women, once opened, this confidence gap fails to close."[6]

I know the confidence gap is real. I saw it with my own daughter, Madeleine, as she moved from elementary school to middle school. We need to take a hard look at why this happens to our daughters and take steps to foster confidence in them. Moreover, we need to foster it in ourselves, especially because others already believe how exceptional we are. At Linkage,

we find women consistently rate themselves significantly lower on our 360°
assessment than their peers or managers rate them.

There is nothing wrong with humility—but our goal is to balance our
humility with confidence so others recognize our competence. We need to
share our accomplishments, stand in our power, and remember: *If you are
in the room, it is because you deserve to be in the room. If you are at the table,
it's because you've earned a seat at the table.* Surround yourself with people
who will remind you of that.

HURDLE 5: BRANDING & PRESENCE

Carla Harris, a senior client advisor at Morgan Stanley and co-chair of
Linkage's Women in Leadership Institute™, has said while keynoting on
our stage for many years, "Perception is the copilot to reality." We need to
seek feedback about how we "land" with others and manage their perceptions. We need to ask ourselves regularly: *Do others see me as I wish to be
seen? Am I making the impact I intend? Am I checking with others to ensure my
intention and impact are aligned?*

Do not allow others to define your brand. It is yours to own. At a recent
staff retreat, we gave our team the following assignment for practice: *identify the three words you want people to use when describing you professionally
when you're not in the room.* As an example, I chose the words "inspiring,"
"committed," and "engaging."

We then asked everyone to share their words in a small group and
get feedback on whether they are "showing up" in a way that aligns with
their intentions.

If carefully selected and curated, these words are your Superpowers—
your strengths and your gifts. They can evolve over time, but only if they
are evident to you and others—and only if you work on making them visible. Most importantly, your brand should feel authentic to you instead of a
forced fit into a mold that doesn't represent you at your core.

Just after that session, one of our product management directors, a man, started a meeting by saying, "I want you all to know that I'm working on bringing my strength around strategic thinking to the forefront. I have been known for that in my previous roles, but not here. So, as we begin to solve this product problem, I'm going to highlight the strategic thinking I've already done and seek your input."

I applauded the explicit way he was managing his brand and practicing the very Superpowers he wanted people to see in him. I have rarely seen a woman do the same.

Women tend to struggle more with identifying and owning their strengths. We often advise women in our development programs to text five people in their close network and ask them to respond with three words that they would use to describe them. It's an easy way to determine how others see you. But regardless of how you discover your brand, women need to diligently manage it, which requires actively reinforcing the brand you want people to associate with you.

HURDLE 6: MAKING THE ASK

How do we ask for what we really want and, just as important, ensure we get it? Part of making the ask is having the clarity to know what we want. Another part is having the confidence to proclaim it to those who can help us get it. (Are you starting to see how the hurdles are tied together?) Making the ask is all about asking for what we *really* want, not the lesser, watered-down version of what we think will play well with the person we are talking to. Gaining this perspective is especially important, as we need to consistently negotiate our time, our roles, our resources, and our flexibility.

One of my team members reached out regarding the virtual school schedule for her preschool-aged son during the initial COVID-19 lockdown. She asked to change her working hours to start at 4 AM so she could tend to his online schooling during the day and alternate shifts with her spouse. I appreciated her creativity, but what she really wanted (and needed) was permission to let go of some work duties—that handful of hours we all have in any given week where we engage in meetings that aren't critical or perform tasks that could be delegated.

That was the ask that would make a real difference for her, rather than trying to rearrange her hours to take on even more work. Yet she seemed reticent to make that specific ask, either because she didn't feel she deserved it or she felt she would be told no. I gave her permission to opt out of any meetings that didn't align with her son's school schedule and welcomed kids and pets to any meetings if it meant she or other colleagues could attend more easily. It wasn't a perfect solution, but through awareness and open communication, we could establish and evolve expectations as the pandemic continued to unfold.

As we rise in our careers, it may not occur to us to ask for what we want. But the sooner we realize that we can, the better. The more often we ask, the more comfortable we get with asking, and the more we learn about how to navigate future asks. Even if we don't get everything we want, we usually get *something*—and it's usually much better than what we get if we don't ask at all.

HURDLE 7: NETWORKING

I spend way more time on networking now than I ever did before. Between utilizing LinkedIn, speaking at conferences, and asking for introductions, I regularly expand, explore, and strengthen my network to build relationships that may be mutually beneficial now or in the future. Earlier in my career, this felt like an onerous chore, even a waste of time. Many times, I was reluctant to put myself out there in circles where there were so few other women. Also, I was busy, working hard to prove myself.

With experience came the courage to make the ask—for that meeting, referral, or advice. I realized that others were as invested in helping me as I was in helping them, but *only* if I made the connection and articulated what

I could offer them and what I hoped I could gain in return. Networking is not always perfectly reciprocal, of course, but I find that giving first makes it easier to leverage your network for specific asks later.

Sarah Breigle leads all our marketing efforts at Linkage, and I connected her to a powerful industry network as an investment in her development. It's a significant annual fee for us, but Sarah has been with us for 15 years, and I want to retain her as a highly valued employee. I also know it's good for Linkage, as it allows her to garner critical external perspectives from time spent with professionals from other organizations. Access to this network has already had a positive impact personally and professionally for Sarah and her team.

It's not enough just to curate a network; we need to consistently nurture and activate it. Based on the clarity you have about your professional future, I challenge you to identify the handful of people who can help you immediately, whether you know them now or not. Write them down. Then, make the ask, even for a 15-minute virtual meeting, and think about what you may be able to offer them in return.

OVERCOMING THE HURDLES TO WOMEN'S ADVANCEMENT

Overcoming the hurdles requires developing specific skills as we gain experience in the workplace. It's an exciting journey of self-discovery and personal development, but it is not a solitary one. Far from it!

While we can recognize and evaluate our own behaviors, it's often helpful to gain the perspectives of other people whom we engage with regularly: direct reports, managers, peers, and even family members. That's why we at Linkage prefer to measure hurdles using our 360° assessments, so you have more awareness about how you see yourself and how others see you.

For now, we are going to explore each of the hurdles in more detail and delve into the specific skills you can cultivate to overcome them. After laying the foundation on how to overcome the Inner Critic, we'll begin each chapter with a brief self-diagnostic so you can see where you currently stand in regard to each hurdle. Once you get a feel for your greatest strengths and biggest growth opportunities, you'll know where to focus your efforts.

There's a lot of ground to cover, but don't be discouraged. We're striving for progress, not perfection. All women have the capacity to become stronger, more effective leaders. We simply need to pursue the experiences that help us grow. As you work to scale the hurdles holding you back, you'll move ever closer to achieving your aspirations and fulfilling your potential as the leader you want to become.

PART TWO

Overcoming the Hurdles

3

Inner Critic—Quiet the Voice of Judgment

The voice in our head can haunt us. All. Day. Long.

You know the voice I mean. For many women, it most often expresses self-judgment. The voice can tear us down; make us question our capabilities; and instill shame, doubt, or fear. It can paralyze us and prevent us from taking action. Its essence is harshness. Ironically, it can also judge others, making us question the value of those around us as a way to build ourselves up.

The name of the voice is the Inner Critic, and as we discussed in the previous chapter, it's an ever-present part of us. However, it can be calmed and coached. We believe that the Inner Critic is so powerful that we position it as the foundational hurdle that weaves its way through the rest and impacts our ability to overcome them.

For example, consider what happens when you're trying to get clear on what you aspire to next as a leader (the Clarity hurdle). You may ask yourself: *Do I want to lead a team through a high-profile project? Innovate the next product my company releases? Find my balance and contribute to the success of my team while still being present as a parent, partner, or friend?* As you start to envision and plan where you want to go and who you want to be, the voice weighs in and takes over.

> *Can you really do that?*
> *You don't have enough experience.*
> *That's too ambitious; you need to be more realistic.*

When left unchecked, the Inner Critic may impact your ability to reach a goal before you even set it.

While we did not coin the term at Linkage, we identified the Inner Critic very early in our work as one of the biggest challenges for women to overcome. A number of self-help books deal with the Inner Critic, and some use other terms to denote it, such as the "Judge" or the "Gremlin." We limit our discussion of the Inner Critic here to the impact it may have on the advancement of a woman leader.

Let's explore how your Inner Critic can impact you and others on your own leadership journey.

WHAT IS THE INNER CRITIC, EXACTLY?

Pause right now and think about the last time you reacted to a situation. It likely occurred within the last hour. Try to recall the inner dialogue that shaped your reaction. Was that voice judging yourself? Someone else? What did the voice sound like, what did it say, and how do you feel about it?

It is important to note here a saying that we use often when discussing the Inner Critic:

> *What you think and feel drives what you say and do.*

The Inner Critic influences our thoughts and our feelings. This, in turn, affects our speech and our actions. Consciously or unconsciously, we react to that voice. When we don't coach the Inner Critic, it can take control and cause us to say something we regret or act in a way that has a negative impact. Going back to your example, what did you say or do as a result of hearing that voice?

The Inner Critic is usually grounded in expectations we place on ourselves and others, which can come from internalized bias. It makes judgments based on what "should" be. That judgment can point in one of two directions—One Down or One Up.

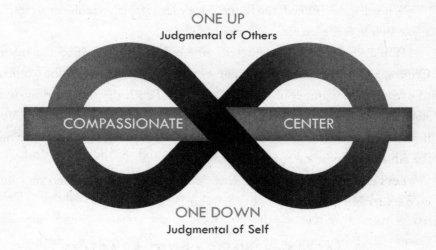

ONE UP
Judgmental of Others

COMPASSIONATE   CENTER

ONE DOWN
Judgmental of Self

One Down judgments target ourselves and our own worth. They can prevent us from opting in, taking the promotion, or stepping into our dreams. These judgments might sound like: *I can't believe I just said that; I sound like an idiot; I don't have enough experience;* or *I don't think it's for me.*

Conversely, *One Up* judgments target others, and they can be more common for executives as we move up in the ranks. In these instances, we believe we are right, given all our experience. A One Up judgment might sound like the following:

* He should know that by now.
* She should have recognized the problem sooner.
* The team should have taken responsibility for the outcomes.

When we hear ourselves "*should*-ing" all over someone, chances are our Inner Critic is in One Up mode.

We can't be the most effective leader—or human—if we are operating from a place of One Up or One Down. If our Inner Critic is constantly and harshly criticizing ourselves or others, we create discord and diminish the value of the people with whom we work. Ultimately, our goal is to be grounded in what Linkage calls *Compassionate Center*, a place where we recognize our own worthiness and the worthiness of others. As the phrase suggests, we show compassion to ourselves and to those around us.

From Compassionate Center we realize that there is enough to go around—enough recognition, enough resources, and enough money—and that we don't have to fight for every scrap or tear others down to make ourselves feel better. This means we can be competent and confident, and we can even "win"—but without feeling superior or treating others like they are inferior to us. We can also be humble and see the value in others without questioning our own worth.

Instead of berating yourself for not getting the promotion over your peer or suggesting that she didn't deserve it, the voice of Compassionate Center sounds like this: "Congratulations on your promotion. I have aspirations to be promoted, too. Could we grab coffee so I can learn about how you achieved that?"

When you are in Compassionate Center, respect is the foundation of communication. When speaking with others, it is about being able to disagree and being open to their point of view. When it is about yourself, it is suspending the "shame game" of how you could have done something better. When I operate from Center, rather than beat myself up, I give myself the same grace and space that I would provide others to fix what might have gone wrong and move forward.

Let's build the capability to operate consistently with compassion.

WHY IS THE INNER CRITIC A HURDLE FOR WOMEN?

We need to understand that both men and women have an Inner Critic, and the practice of coaching the Inner Critic is valuable to all of us. Men can be as judgmental of themselves and others as women can be. The difference here, grounded in our leadership lens, is that the impact of the Inner Critic on the advancement of men is different—it doesn't hold them back like it does women.

Consider this: A recent study by LinkedIn found that new opportunities entice both men and women equally.[1] A similar percentage of both groups are open to exploring new roles, and both viewed a similar number of jobs. As with the outcome of the study discussed in the previous chapter, the difference is that men are more likely to apply. We attribute this phenomenon to the Inner Critic and internalized bias, which leads women to opt out before even trying. Their Inner Critic tells them they don't have all the qualifications, they aren't ready, or they won't get it anyway.

Additionally, the study found that, compared to men, women are 26 percent less likely to ask for a referral. It's easy to imagine the voice saying, *I don't want to inconvenience anyone* or, *It's not appropriate to ask a client for a favor.* Unfortunately, the impact of women opting out is compounded by real external bias, as evidenced by recruiters being 13 percent less likely to click on a woman's profile when she shows up in their searches.

As we've already learned, our Inner Critic and its judgments about what "should be" are formed by what we see and hear around us, from our parents, teachers, colleagues, and the media. Women may not see a path to their goals because no one who looks like us has shown us the way before. With so few role models, the Inner Critic becomes a natural default: *I can't do it, because no one else has* or, *It's too hard to be the first.* The concept of "you have to see it to believe it" has weight.

This is why when Hillary Clinton was running for president, and especially when Kamala Harris was elected vice president, a lot of media portrayed girls and multicultural children reacting with joy. *Finally,* people who looked like them were in the most powerful roles in the nation. Yet, despite these incredible breakthroughs, women have a lot of catching up to do before it feels normal rather than newsworthy for us to be in those leadership positions.

There are still far too many "firsts" for women on our collective journey toward gender equity, especially when you consider women of color and other intersections of identity, like sexual orientation or disability. In October 2022, there was large-scale media coverage of the first Native American woman in space. While there are many firsts still to come, more continue to be recognized as important examples to the next generations.

The impact of catching up in a world that didn't originally envision you in the roles you fill today is significant. It leaves women constantly questioning who and how to be, second-guessing ourselves and wanting to fit in instead of making waves. The reality is that none of us can bring our authentic selves into the workplace and be fully engaged if assimilation to the leadership majority is the only way to succeed. As we will discuss in the next chapter, the Inner Critic is the voice of our internalized bias, especially when it comes to what we should or shouldn't do. We have to first coach that voice and then challenge our own biases to continue our evolution as leaders.

This burden of the Inner Critic is not unique to women, but it *is* uniquely getting in our way, and we will help you find a way to identify it and coach it back to Compassionate Center.

WHAT HAS CHANGED IN THE LAST FEW YEARS?

The Inner Critic is more likely to be triggered when we are stressed, and the last few years have given us plenty to stress about. The good news is that this has resulted in a much-needed increase in awareness and focus on critical issues like mental health, social justice, and inclusion. The bad news is that all this combined pressure of facing these issues makes it more likely that we'll go One Up or One Down with greater frequency and greater bounce.

While there are many factors at play, there are a few that have had an outsized impact on our current reality: the emergence of the "Now" culture, followed by the immediate blurring of all boundaries during the COVID-19 pandemic. We'll address "Now" culture first.

For the last two decades, we have been immersed in a world of rapidly accelerating innovation; instantaneous communication; and the ability to easily access information, goods, and services globally. Perhaps the best example of this is Amazon Prime's promise of next-day and even same-day service for millions of products. Way back in 2005, Amazon Prime became a membership with two-day delivery. Six years later, they added the on-demand Amazon Prime Video, followed by same-day delivery in over 27 metro areas. In 2019, they added grocery delivery.

Not only have technological advancements completely shifted our expectations around delivery of goods and services, but they've also impacted the expectations of how we perform at work. The assumption is we can get more done faster, with no pauses and no delays. In the midst of all the urgency, there is little time to prioritize or let go of responsibilities. Triggered by all this pressure, the Inner Critic speaks loudly at home and at work: *Does anyone see how hard I'm working? When will I achieve enough? When will I be enough?*

With that evolution of expectations as a backdrop, COVID-19 hit, and the life we had grown accustomed to jerked to a halt. By early April 2020, almost everyone's job had changed. There were new expectations, hours, safety precautions, reporting structures, and social norms. But for many of us, the most difficult transition was working virtually from our homes. It didn't take long for the world to finally bear witness to and acknowledge the disproportionate burden on women once their families were schooling, working, and eating every meal under the same roof. While it had always been a struggle for women to manage all the pieces, our world tumbled down when the pandemic erupted.

A woman I know had two kids who were sent home from school with school-provided laptops that fateful Friday. The same day, her boss told her to take her computer home as well, declaring that everyone would move to remote work. Separately, her husband's job required he still go into the office. Every day, she had to juggle making sure her kids were getting logged in and joining their virtual school, helping them when needed, making breakfast and lunch, and then managing her team of ten, each of whom had their own challenges. When her husband returned each night, she had to figure out dinner as well because that had always been her role.

She was bouncing between One Up and One Down. The voice in her head judged her spouse: *Why doesn't he see how hard I am working? He should step up.* It also judged herself: *I have failed as a mom—I can't protect my kids or help them enough with their schoolwork* and *There is no way my team has faith in me with all this noise and distraction in the background.* Chaos and overwhelm is the Inner Critic's playground, and it was hard to even slow down enough to become aware of how loud it had become. All our energy was focused on surviving.

During this time and for the few years that followed, it was easy to judge others for almost anything: wearing a mask, not wearing one, being the source of the last outbreak at work or school, having it "easy" because *They get to still go to an office* or *She doesn't have kids*, and on and on. We also judged ourselves, especially as we renegotiated our home life, whether we were married with kids and fielding the responsibilities that fell on us, or single and trapped inside with decreasing hope that we'd ever get to go out again. That voice nagged, *Why can't you do it all?* or, *Why can't you be like Alex; she has it all together?* or, *Why did you put your mother in that nursing home where she's now trapped with no visitors?* All these expectations led to exhaustion, burnout, and frustration.

When we consider the increased stress that fuels the Inner Critic, we can see the impact not only on ourselves but also on those we lead. If, as a leader, I hold myself to an impossible standard and become judgmental (One Up) about how everyone else is not upholding the same standards, I will burn out my team and hurt the very relationships I rely on. If I can coach my Inner Critic, I will acknowledge my stress in the moment, identify that I am One Upping, and coach her down to Center before mandating to a direct report, "Do whatever it takes to get it done!"

We have created a requirement of acceleration—of everything. To overcome this, we have to face each other as humans, not numbers or resources, and have real conversations, with the most senior of us aligned and leading the discussion. These past few years have taken us on a wild ride, but no two people were impacted the same way. Your journey is unique to you, and as you consider coaching your Inner Critic, focus on whether your behaviors resulting from One Up or One Down judgments are currently impeding your path to greatness. Let's discover how.

THE INNER CRITIC IN REAL LIFE

In the chapters to come, I will generally start this section by telling my own story about how I was confronted by the specific hurdle and how I overcame it. This time, though, I want to start with an explanation of Linkage's four-step model that will help you coach your Inner Critic and vault over the rest of the hurdles.

You can use this on your own, or you can work with a friend or coach. Just remember this is *your* journey, and it is about controlling the factors you can while knowing there are others you cannot. We can't change another individual, and we certainly can't single-handedly change our organizational culture or society. But we can own and influence our Inner Critic and coach it to help us develop into the leader we aspire to be.

Shannon Bayer leads our revenue team at Linkage on top of being our resident expert and keynote speaker on the Inner Critic. Earlier in her leadership, she couldn't understand the value of coaching the Inner Critic in a situation where she knew she was right. She asked, "Why do I have to be in Compassionate Center when I am just trying to explain that I am right?" What finally clicked for her was that being right doesn't mean much if you sacrifice the relationship, either at work or at home.

The skill of coaching your Inner Critic is central to creating, maintaining, and growing work relationships, which in turn grows your credibility and ability to be trusted as a leader. When we are in Compassionate Center, we can lead difficult situations and conversations with respect. It is in these defining moments that we emerge in our full potential.

Here are the steps to coaching your Inner Critic. The more you use them, the better and faster you will get at acknowledging her voice, preventing the extreme bounce to One Up or One Down, and moving back to Compassionate Center.

BECOME AWARE
Notice your inner critic.

PUSH PAUSE
Stop doing and start thinking!

BE COMPASSIONATE
Be kind to yourself and others.

GET CURIOUS
Ask yourself, "What's going on here?"

Become Aware

It may seem simple, but the first step to coaching your Inner Critic is to become aware of her activity in your body. Awareness is simple in concept but hard in practice.

Recently, a member of our marketing team emailed Shannon to congratulate her on a job well done on a large webinar. The marketing manager relayed how badly she felt about not capturing a specific image with Shannon and her guest. She was spiraling into One Down when Shannon picked up the phone and said, "Thank you for your email, but please don't go One Down for a simple thing like a graphic. You are amazing at your job; don't spend another minute thinking about this." The manager laughed and said, "I didn't even realize I was doing it until you told me." We won't always have someone we trust there to blow the whistle, so it is up to us to identify the signs when our Inner Critic acts out.

Awareness can come from studying yourself and your reactions. Try to catch the thoughts in your head, notice your body language, and tune in to the emotion of your reaction. When I am triggered into One Up, I am usually readying myself to explain why the other person is wrong, even as they are still making their point. My heart races; I talk more quickly; I interrupt. When I am in One Down, I physically and emotionally withdraw, stop listening, and sometimes check out or shut down completely.

The Inner Critic, especially when she manifests as One Down, can keep you up at night as you play over and over in your head what you did or didn't do. It can also cause you to look to others to reassure you, but until you quiet your Inner Critic, none of their praise will help.

If becoming aware seems challenging at first, you can start by looking backward. At first, you may notice your Inner Critic only after you've said something you regret. Remember, what you think and feel drives what you say and do. Take that experience and identify the first thoughts or feelings that triggered you and the actions that followed. Once you identify observable behaviors, ask a peer or friend to help you the next time they notice it. Come up with a signal that you can share to become aware. The more you practice catching your Inner Critic, the easier it gets.

Push Pause

Once you are aware you are going One Up or One Down, you must pause. Again, this is easy in concept but much harder in practice. How can we pause in the middle of a cross-functional meeting or a heated budget discussion? By trying not to react until you've reached Compassionate Center, which is the next step.

Consider this example: When I started at Linkage, Shannon had already been assigned to an important special project for more than a year. Intended to create a new revenue stream, the initiative had full support from the board and Rick Pumfrey, our COO. I realized there had been significant time and resources already sunk into this project, but I had some experience with that business model and doubted we would be able to make it work. When I met with Shannon and her team to learn more, I questioned the value of the effort and whether we should continue to pursue it.

Understandably, Shannon's Inner Critic shot to One Up. This was important work she was leading in partnership with Rick, so my comments must have felt like a direct attack on them both. The discussion started to get tense, but, to Shannon's credit, she paused and said, "I am not sure what I say will be productive right now. Would it be okay if we discussed it more later when I have a chance to come up with scenarios on how we might move forward?" By pressing pause, she stopped the escalating conversation. We met again a few days later and agreed to let the plan play out for the rest of the year. If we didn't have momentum by then, we agreed to shelve the project.

If you don't have the luxury of leaving a meeting and starting over later, you can also try this: "I just need a moment to frame what I want to say. Can you give me a minute?" The direct ask is the easiest way to pause, but if that's not comfortable, the indirect ask can be more subtle. If you're in a meeting, you can pause by taking a bathroom break, stepping out to refill your drink, turning off your camera if on a video call, or dropping your pen under the desk and taking a deep breath while you retrieve it. If you are in a recurring situation, like a weekly meeting, during which you know you will be triggered, connect with a trusted partner in the meeting and let them know that you need their help to push pause when they see the triggering situation arise by finding a way to take the spotlight off you for a minute or two.

I made a huge mistake in my first annual business review with our all-male private equity board of directors by grading our overall results like a high school teacher from A through F and presenting them on a slide during our quarterly meeting. Our transformation efforts were in full swing, but our financials were not yet where we needed them to be. After a year, it was time for me to take accountability. I had given us a D on our "financial turnaround" goal, when one of my board members began what I perceived to be an all-out attack and graded the turnaround a complete failure—a solid F—along with my lack of ownership of it.

I felt myself sliding quickly into One Down. I was berating myself for even putting up a score sheet to begin with. My Inner Critic took over: *Why hadn't I just color-coded the objectives red/yellow/green? Why didn't I acknowledge my failure before he pointed it out in front of everyone? I'm only one year into this role, and at this rate, I'm not going to make it much longer.* I felt the tears coming, so I called for a bathroom break. When I emerged, I had a quick hallway check-in with Rick, the only other Linkage executive in the room. We agreed to change the course of the meeting and shift to the next year's growth strategy instead of rehashing the previous year's performance. The pause was what I needed to reset.

Be Compassionate

The goal is to move from One Up or One Down to Compassionate Center as quickly as possible. This is a place where you are no longer emotional or reactive, and it is best to pause as long as you need to get there. As the name suggests, *compassion* is the secret. If you are One Up, find compassion for the other person; if you are One Down, find compassion for yourself.

Let's start with One Up. Finding compassion for others means realizing that the value of the relationship is much higher than the value of proving yourself right. This can be a tough concept, especially for women who have been working hard to be heard and for their competence to be recognized. Demonstrating compassion for others entails finding connection and remembering why your relationship has value, even if it isn't always evident.

Summon an Inner Coach to help your Inner Critic get from your One Up state back down to Center. Discover your Coach's personality—is it your own voice of reason gently urging you to calm down? A parent's tone reminding you of the Golden Rule? Think of the kindest, gentlest, most compassionate person you've ever met, and give your Inner Coach that voice. When you know your Inner Critic is causing you to react, blow the whistle, stop play, and call in your Coach to help.

Your Inner Coach can help in two ways—generally or contextually. Your Coach can have a general mantra that gets you to Center regardless of the situation. Mine is one my mother repeated often throughout my life: "Do you want to be right, or do you want to be happy?" Shannon's is: "I am not perfect and neither are they, but we are both trying."

There are likely specific people or situations that trigger you, requiring your Coach to be more contextual. This may take a bit of planning, and you need to determine exactly what your relationship is with those people or situations, how you need to encounter them over time, and what strategies to implement when you begin to react.

I love the story Shannon tells of a former coworker who was driven to perform at any cost, steamrolling others and leaving bodies in her wake. While all their interactions were challenging, Shannon learned to find compassion by thinking of the things they had in common before she was triggered into One Up—children of a similar age, love for great food, and passion around advancing women leaders. Before every call, Shannon took one minute to remember their points of connection and reminded herself, "I am not perfect, and she is not perfect, but we are both trying." That helped her get down to Compassionate Center even before the conversation started. Shannon maintained a strong working relationship while protecting her own leadership brand as well. If others observe you repeatedly in your One Up peak, it not only creates a negative impact on the person you are judging, but it will also impact how others view you.

Now let's address One Down, where you must find compassion for yourself. One Down is harder to coach because while we understand intellectually the need to find value and connection in the relationships we need from others, women especially tend to discount their own value. Our Linkage data, for example, proves that women underrate themselves consistently on our assessments compared to how all their other raters perceive them.

So, when we become aware and pause when we are in One Down, we need to create a path back up to Center with a supportive Inner Coach who challenges us to focus not on what is wrong with us but on what is right and what is possible.

To get out of One Down, first identify the voice of your critic and the resulting feeling—ashamed, unworthy, angry, etc. For example, sometimes I replay something I said or did in an important meeting and question it immediately: *Did I really add any value? Did I look like a fool? Was it a mistake to raise that point at all?* Then, I play it out again and again, sharing it with others and making it even bigger with my obsession: "My boss was in the room, my team saw me flounder, my future is at risk." The rehashing continues, and it is now past the time to call in the Inner Coach to intervene.

Observe the emotion if you can—in this case, humiliation—and then find the words your Coach needs to provide. Here is the gentle voice I summon: *During that meeting, you managed a well-thought agenda, facilitated a difficult conversation, and got approval for additional funding. Either address it or let it go, but don't dwell on it; you aren't perfect, and you'll have another chance to try again.* Your Inner Coach will recognize when you are swirling in One Down, point out what you do well, and identify a way forward.

While it may seem obvious that One Up can be seen by others and impact your brand, so can One Down. If you seek validation in your shame, your anger, or your lack of value, that will eventually become your brand—someone who doubts herself or doesn't feel "good enough." That is just as detrimental as the leader running around trying to prove they are smarter than everyone else in the room.

Get Curious

Once you have become aware, paused, and moved back to Center, you are no longer reacting but instead taking the time to become curious about the situation in order to respond to it more thoughtfully. Most of the time when our Inner Critic is triggered, we are around others—in a meeting or a conversation. That means we can ask questions that not only help us focus on the topic at hand but also possibly give us more information that will help us respond compassionately. Find out more about the other person's perspective and needs. Make sure you are really at Center and seeking to understand versus posing questions you already have answers to. Make your questions open-ended and actively listen to how the other person responds. Here are some examples of questions that can move an otherwise difficult conversation forward:

* ✳ I can see we are coming at this from different angles; how did you decide this is the best course of action?
* ✳ What do you think is possible based on what we know today?
* ✳ What is our best next step to move forward together?

If appropriate, you can also make explicit what is happening internally. "I'm having trouble listening, so I'm going to pause for a moment before I react again. I'd like to learn more about your thought process."

THE INNER COACH AT WORK

Learning to coach my Inner Critic helped me salvage some of my most important professional relationships with my board of directors. After what I believed was a banner year emerging from the COVID-19 crisis, I joined a virtual performance review with three board members, and I was excited to hear their reflections. I expected them to congratulate me on my leadership and a job well done, but instead, in the interest of time, they narrowed right in on two areas of concern they had identified as flaws.

I couldn't believe it. My Inner Critic went straight to One Up. I felt punished, and instead of pausing, I lashed out, offering my own unsolic- ited perspective of their leadership and introducing new requests to protect myself and my executive team. They escalated in kind, and when I realized there was no good path forward after 30 minutes, I ended the call abruptly. Across the next day or two, I replayed the event repeatedly in my head and with several important people in my network, trying to diagnose how it had gone so wrong.

Then, I called in my Inner Coach.

As I reflected, I became more aware of my Inner Critic and how quickly I had reacted. It took me awhile to pause and return to Compassionate Center, but I eventually realized that we all were striving for the same goal to run a successful business with the best possible outcomes during the critical year ahead, when we planned to sell the company.

I realized there was an opening for a "do-over" given the unresolved tension, and I needed to make the first move. I crafted a long email that started with this:

> I realize we were all disappointed and frustrated by the call last week, but there's nothing more important for me than to be completely aligned and committed to the best possible outcome for the board and the executive team as we move toward the sale of the company. I don't feel like we're there right now, but we're not that far away.

I went on to craft my recommendation on the path forward, reopening the major points of discussion that had shut down in the last conversation. Before sending the email, I picked up the phone and talked through every point with the board chair. The tension was released—he thanked me for the outreach, and we both apologized for the way the performance review was handled.

It took me a few days, and it was hard. But each time I use the four steps to coach my Inner Critic, I get a little better.

We'll now move to the "Act Now" section, which will appear at the end of each of our hurdle chapters to help you apply the principles we've discussed to your own life and leadership. Think of these as a helpful guide to support you in planning for your own next steps on your leadership journey. We also recommend reading this book with a friend or book club to talk through the implications of what we hope you are learning about yourself.

✳ ACT NOW
How to Calm the Inner Critic

Here are a few things you can do immediately:

1. Get a peer coach to help you build awareness of your Inner Critic and pause when either of you notice the Critic taking over.
2. Write in a journal after heated conversations to work through what you can do to repair the relationship and respond more thoughtfully next time. Identify the thoughts and feelings that led to your reactive words and actions.
3. Come up with a mantra to coach your Inner Critic back to Compassionate Center.
4. Celebrate small wins and milestones. For example, note when you pause and stop escalating.

Above all, be kind to yourself. No matter how much effort you put in, you will not be able to permanently quiet your Inner Critic. With practice, however, you will reduce the inclination to react from a place of One Up or One Down using words or actions that you will regret later. The goal is to become aware more quickly in these situations so that you can more often pause before reacting—finding compassion for yourself and others and reducing the pain you could cause for either.

It is never too soon or too late to start this practice.

Now, to help you become aware and prioritize which hurdles are your biggest strengths and challenges, we invite you to take a brief self-assessment at **SHRM.org/InHerOwnVoice.** At the beginning of each chapter, we have posed the question from this assessment related to that specific hurdle. Take a moment before starting each chapter to reflect and choose the option that best represents how you demonstrate each hurdle. We also encourage you to discuss these questions with others who know you well, ideally in a professional context. The goal is to increase your scores over time.

4

Internal Bias—Discard the Deeply Held Beliefs That No Longer Serve You

RATE YOURSELF (1–5)

In day-to-day work as a leader, I . . .					
Am open-minded or unlimited in thinking about my own capability and potential to achieve.					
Rarely Demonstrate 1	Sometimes Demonstrate 2	Often Demonstrate 3	Very Often Demonstrate 4	Almost Always Demonstrate 5	N/A
○	○	○	○	○	○

How open-minded are you in thinking about your capabilities and potential to achieve? Your thinking may be unlimited, like when you were a child and believed anything was possible. Or it may be shut down completely, with a belief that destiny has dealt you a certain hand of cards and you are stuck with them. Your perspective will be greatly influenced by the messages you received from the external environment you were immersed in from birth. Those environmental impacts can be extreme. For example, when was the last time you decided not to go after something—a promotion, a stretch assignment, a new job? Whose "voice" stopped you?

Maybe it was the parent who told you not to set your sights too high or to stand out. Maybe it was your community, in which you were the "first" (first of your gender, race, ethnicity, or sexuality) and internalized that "people like you" didn't get those jobs, so you had to work harder and perform better than anyone else to prove yourself. Maybe it was a professor who subtly reinforced the idea that men had the "harder" business and analytic skills and women excelled in "softer" creative pursuits like marketing and communication.

For whatever reason, you opted out of an opportunity before you gave yourself a chance to pursue it. You're not alone. We all internalize the biases that exist externally, and they permeate our thoughts and influence our actions. They don't necessarily determine our destiny—but we have to become aware of them and consciously challenge them if we're to rise above the limits they impose.

For me, opting out wasn't a big issue. Ever since I was a kid, I've always thrown myself into bigger challenges than I was prepared for—at home, school, or work—and it's served me pretty well throughout my career and life. I was raised to believe that I could achieve anything I set out to do, so I'll never forget when my dad recommended that I quit the high school basketball team my junior year. My coach didn't see the same potential in me that I saw in myself, and I was distraught, game after game, when I didn't get the playing time. Yet I was even more incensed by the suggestion to quit, and it motivated me to double down and prove both my father and coach wrong. When the Winter Park Wildcats won the state championship my senior year, I was named the MVP.

Instead, I have a different internal bias that continues to haunt me and bring its own challenges. It's the voice that whispers, *You can do it all if you work hard enough. And if you do it all yourself, the results will be better.* That belief was fine when I was a student, working hard to get good grades all the way through graduate school. Even through my twenties—before I managed large teams, before I was married, before I had kids—I could mostly hold it all together and make it work through sheer force of will. Even after I became a manager, wife, and mother, there were many days, even weeks and months and years, when it seemed I was performing well on all cylinders—and people saw me that way, too.

However, here is my lesson in this lifetime: The belief that I can do it all myself is a limiting one. All this "doing" interferes with being present for those relationships that mean the most to me. It also prevents others from stepping in to help, especially if they feel they can't meet my expectations for how things should be done. And mostly, working harder and trying to "do it all" doesn't ultimately lead to finding purpose and joy. I realize now, a few decades and many leadership roles later, that I will never reach my own bar of feeling like I have done enough, well enough. I have gotten better about recognizing this deep internal bias, especially when I catch my Inner Critic judging me—or others—for stopping to rest.

One of my mentors is Marshall Goldsmith, who is one of the world's most renowned leadership coaches and experts. He helped me understand that achievement and happiness are independent variables. Since I will never achieve enough to be satisfied, I'm working to change my belief by focusing on happiness in the moment and celebrating achievements along the way.

We've all got something to work on, so whatever your limiting beliefs, the goal is to identify those that may be barriers to success in your career and life. Those beliefs no longer serve you.

WHAT IS INTERNAL BIAS, EXACTLY?

As discussed in chapter one, we are surrounded by contexts and cultures that reflect many external biases. From a young age, we take in all of this as data—the voices, images, and experiences from our homes, media, schools, and offices. We might observe, *I see mostly men at the top of the organization.* And then we add meaning to the data: *Men have always been the majority in leadership since I've been here.* This is where internal bias begins.

From there, we make assumptions (*Men will always be favored to get the leadership roles here*), draw conclusions (*I probably shouldn't even consider it since I'm not a man*), and form beliefs (*I can't make it to the top here*). Operating from those beliefs, we act, generally looking for information that confirms our beliefs (*I'm not going for the job because I don't have what they are looking for*).

This internalized bias results in a cognitive shortcut that we rely on to make decisions. It happens quickly and largely unconsciously, and this internal bias fuels our Inner Critic, which tells us we can't do the job or we shouldn't even try.

The entire cycle moves us quickly from a piece of data—a fact, comment, or observation—through a mental process to a conclusion. This cycle was best illustrated back in 1970 by management theorist Chris Argyris, who coined it the "Ladder of Inference." The model has endured for more than 50 years because it's a tool that helps us make our thinking explicit and better understand our own beliefs as well as those of others. It is still so relevant today because despite our evolution as humans, we are still at our core weighed down by the primitive nature of our minds. It is very hard to change these inborn processes—mostly because we aren't aware of our own thinking that guides our beliefs and actions.

The Ladder of Inference helps us gain awareness of our internal biases in order to make changes in our thoughts and actions. There's a very real example on page 67: start from the bottom of the ladder and work your way up.

The focus of Internal Bias is how our own biases impact the choices we make. These are our own self-limiting beliefs. Once we identify those biases, we can analyze them, determine the impact, and, if negative, overcome them and move forward.

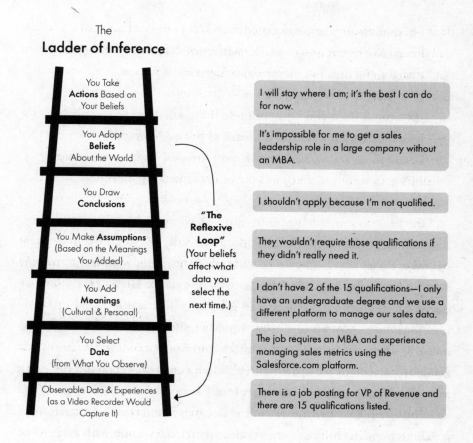

The
Ladder of Inference

You Take **Actions** Based on Your Beliefs

I will stay where I am; it's the best I can do for now.

You Adopt **Beliefs** About the World

It's impossible for me to get a sales leadership role in a large company without an MBA.

You Draw **Conclusions**

I shouldn't apply because I'm not qualified.

"The Reflexive Loop" (Your beliefs affect what data you select the next time.)

You Make **Assumptions** (Based on the Meanings You Added)

They wouldn't require those qualifications if they didn't really need it.

You Add **Meanings** (Cultural & Personal)

I don't have 2 of the 15 qualifications—I only have an undergraduate degree and we use a different platform to manage our sales data.

You Select **Data** (from What You Observe)

The job requires an MBA and experience managing sales metrics using the Salesforce.com platform.

Observable Data & Experiences (as a Video Recorder Would Capture It)

There is a job posting for VP of Revenue and there are 15 qualifications listed.

WHY IS INTERNAL BIAS A HURDLE FOR WOMEN?

Despite the many decades of effort toward the gender equality movement, societal expectations grounded in bias and assumptions continue to have a lasting and substantial impact. The focus has been primarily on external bias, but in 2014, Orange Grove Consulting first published its research on women's internalized bias. Its work focused on identifying self-imposed barriers to success for high-potential women, such as wanting to be liked, doing it all alone, and perfectionism. The study codified many of the most common barriers,[1] which come from our deeply held beliefs and feed our Inner Critic:

"I have to be nice to be accepted."

"I need to smile more, or people will think I am mad all the time."

"I need to be firm but not abrasive to get what I want."

"I can have it all (or do it all)."

"If I want it done right, I have to do it myself."

"I shouldn't show emotion if I want to be taken seriously."

"I can't show any weakness, only perfection, if I want to succeed."

"I have to work twice as hard to get the same as 'them.'"

The biases we internalize start early, at home and in the community, and are reinforced everywhere we turn, especially in the media and entertainment industries. In the last decade, there has been significant progress made in awareness of gender bias, partly due to actor Geena Davis and her Geena Davis Institute on Gender in Media,[2] which was founded in 2004. Linkage invited her to cochair our annual Women in Leadership Institute™ in 2015, where we learned of her passion in understanding the impact of gender representation disparities in children's entertainment and her drive to work with the industry to impact immediate change.

The Geena Davis Institute's initial research found that three quarters of speaking parts in children's entertainment are male, along with 83 percent of narrators. In group scenes, only 17 percent of the characters are female.[3] Men are shown as leaders in high-level jobs, while women are office assistants. Girls and women are shown most often in the background or in supporting roles. Through the media's portrayal of women as inferior, we have taught countless generations of children to have unconscious gender bias before they can even walk.

Davis's institute has worked to change this across nearly two decades, and its studies in 2020 showed that in family-rated films, we have finally reached gender parity in lead roles and in broader character representation. The Geena Davis Inclusion Quotient (GD-IQ) and Spellcheck for Bias are two new tools that use face and voice recognition to measure gender representation, screen time, and speaking time using machine learning and human coding. The tools can also measure other diversity metrics like race, disability, LGBTQIA+ identity, or body type. This technology helps studios uncover bias and gain feedback so they can influence scripts before they go into production.

Significant victories are *The Hunger Games* and *Brave*, 2012 films that depict strong females as warriors and heroes, wielding their archery bows much like Geena Davis did when she became a semifinalist in the US Olympic trials at the age of 43! Those films drove archery to become a more popular sport for girls than boys for the first time.

What happens in the fictional world plays out in the real world. In partnership with J. Walter Thompson, the institute led a survey a few years ago of 4,300 women in nine countries and found that 58 percent of women said strong women portrayed in TV and film inspired them to be more ambitious; 16 percent took up a new sport; 12 percent left abusive relationships; and 11 percent increased their education.[4]

While these examples offer enormous hope and promise, we know this improved reality has not yet fully impacted the current generations in the workforce. Moving from entertainment to the classroom, these biases still follow us and impact our actions. A 2018 University of Cambridge study showed that women in college are two and a half times less likely to ask questions in class than men.[5] Why? The study cited the "disease to please" or "apology" culture that women have internalized up to that point. They either do not feel "clever enough," "couldn't work up the nerve," or "worried that [they] had misunderstood the content."

The conclusion of the Cambridge study is disappointing but not unexpected. In Europe, while women earn 59 percent of the undergraduate degrees, they earn less than half the PhD diplomas and only 21 percent of senior faculty positions.

If we are less assertive in the classroom, that naturally extends to the workplace, where we remain cautious. It's evident in the language women often lead with when asking a question or offering a comment: "This may be a stupid idea . . ." or, "I'm sorry if this has already been answered . . . ."

When women are conditioned to be sweet and silent and men are rewarded for being bold, we naturally see a shrinking number of women step forward to lead. Even worse, they may be held back from promotional opportunities because they are perceived as "not assertive enough."

While internal bias is not limited to women, men's biases have been formed in a world that allows and encourages men to succeed, specifically white men in the US business culture. For example, for hundreds—if not thousands—of years, tall, strong, athletic men globally have been considered "better." Men who don't have these characteristics may also internalize doubt about their ability to succeed at the highest levels.

Women have taken notice of this societal ideal and acted accordingly. When you analyze CEOs today, both men and women are more likely to have been competitive athletes at the collegiate level.[6] While surprising on the surface that 96 percent of C-suite women played sports, it's likely that this very type of activity helps women overcome their own internal bias by teaching them how to be aggressive, competitive, and eager to take on more responsibility. "Put me in, Coach!"

So, in this way, women have internalized the external bias of aggression and competitiveness as success factors of CEOs, which has been reinforced in the hiring process. This is where external and internal bias meet. Women who have learned how to behave more like the traditional stereotype of successful male leaders are in fact the ones who have risen to the top.

It's complicated, nuanced, and difficult to change—but change starts with our own understanding of how we have internalized the bias that exists around us from a very early age. This is also where organizations have the most power and opportunity to course correct with the current workforce of rising professional women. We need to impact both the external and internal biases today in the business world. We can do so by creating opportunities for both leaders and organizations to reflect on and measure where bias may provide one group an advantage over another and by challenging ourselves and our organizations to change.

WHAT HAS CHANGED IN THE LAST FEW YEARS?

The dramatic changes in the world during the COVID-19 pandemic created more stress but also opened more opportunity to challenge our internal biases. It became a lot harder, if not impossible, to operate with an internal bias that tells us to "act more like the leadership majority" or "withhold our emotion because it might make leaders uncomfortable." The pandemic lifted the curtain on what many women had been trying to hide to fulfill a male model of leadership, complete with the visible impact of house care, childcare, elder care, and staff care. Life was messier, and suddenly the full spectrum of that reality was exposed. From a physical perspective, there was equity in everyone appearing on a screen from their homes, dressed differently from "standard" office attire. And from an emotional perspective, it became more normalized to talk about what was really happening and the toll it was taking on all of us, at work and at home. Women could step into their full authenticity and stop hiding important aspects of themselves and their lives. The window cracked open, allowing us—perhaps even forcing us—to bring more of our Superpowers to our leadership.

It is a perfect time to question whether the belief that "I can't be myself at work" is really serving you. What are different assumptions and conclusions you could make instead, which would lead to different beliefs and actions?

Consider Emmy award–winning journalist Marilu Galvez, president and general manager of WABC-TV in New York. In the fall of 2022, Shannon, Linkage's head of revenue, hosted a webinar with her, and the conversation hovered around the theme of authenticity in the workplace, with Marilu describing how she had spent most of her career feeling that she couldn't show up as her true self at work. They explored Marilu's internal bias from growing up in a multigenerational Latino family surrounded by strong women. Shannon asked her what had changed as she progressed in her career, and Marilu answered that finally, as the most senior leader in her business, she can walk into a room and completely and authentically embrace her full self and personality, complete with her natural hair, voice, dress, and gestures.

Shannon then asked what advice she would give to the most junior woman in the room. Marilu responded immediately: "In the last two years, the entire world has changed, and we can now be seen for who we are. We can also ask for help, as people are more willing to offer it than they ever were before."

Our advice? Recognize that this is a unique moment in time, during which you can ask for what you want and seek out support in whatever form you need. Limit your perfectionism and try more things. Give yourself permission to show up authentically.

Despite the additional stressors across the past few years, there is now more opportunity to stop and shift our outdated assumptions and beliefs, those internal biases preventing us from reaching our full potential as women and as leaders.

INTERNAL BIAS IN REAL LIFE

Let's go back to a few decades ago when my "you can do it all yourself" bias began to break down.

When I was engaged to be married, I shared my vision for child-rearing with Chip, who has now been my partner for 25 years. It was important to me that we balance our parenting roles, and I wanted any future kids to experience their mother and father equally as engaged parents. I expressed my hope that when the day came, each of us would work a four-day workweek, with one day dedicated for us individually to care for the kids, requiring a nanny or alternative childcare for only three days a week. Chip is an agreeable guy, so he listened openly and nodded, as if that were a fine arrangement. In retrospect, however, I realize it seemed like a perfectly plausible plan only to me.

A few years later, we agreed it was time to expand our family, and when we were expecting, I reintroduced the plan I believed we had agreed to. At the time, I was a global consultant with a fair amount of flexibility, so I felt a four-day workweek would be possible. I asked Chip how he planned to manage his schedule to care for our daughter one day each week. It quickly became clear to me that our agreement was "in principle" and not a shared commitment. He was a corporate banker at a traditional financial institution in an era when there was never any talk of paternity leave, let alone a man changing his work schedule to accommodate for childcare. The truth was that he had no intention of asking his employer to be an exception and risk his career ascension.

When Madeleine was born, he dove headfirst into fatherhood but took less than the allotted one week of leave and went back to work. I will never forget the first Monday morning as a parent. I was in bed, exhausted after being up through the night, trying to figure out the rhythms of the nursing, diapers, and feeding. I watched as Chip got up, showered, got dressed, kissed us goodbye, and walked out the door. From what I could tell, his life had changed very little—but mine was transformed.

Now that our three kids are older, I can more clearly see the internal biases at play. Chip's bias was that he was a breadwinner, fulfilling the role he had always seen men play. He was an incredible and caring father, but his beliefs of what caregiving looked like were shaped by his own upbringing, with women raising the children. My bias was "I can do it all on my own," so I worked hard to continue to find success in my career with a flexible schedule while also managing much of the emotional and physical load of the childcare. The pace continued to speed up, and I jumped right on the hamster wheel, believing, *I've got this!*

I carried on with my own four-day workweek plan for the next eight years, working a flexible schedule as a consultant. I knew many other women doing the same thing, trying our best to manage our careers, kids, and homes. Some of us had supportive husbands who pitched in during nights and weekends, enabling us to keep pace with our jobs, but many others had their careers sidelined when they chose to stay home.

These internal biases run deep. Since the beginning of our cave-dwelling days, men have been expected to leave the home and get to work. Until recently, having a child was a good reason for them to take off a few days but not any significant amount of time. Even now that paternity benefits have improved, men in the United States rarely take full advantage of the policies because it "looks bad" at the office. According to Adrienne Schweer of the Bipartisan Policy Center's Task Force on Paid Family Leave, "Men tend not to take leave because they see the impact it has on a woman's career and earnings, they see how the absence causes someone else to pick up additional work to fill in and they don't feel their leadership supports them in taking the leave."[7] While the core of the problem is about giving men opportunity and access to paid leave programs, it is equally about changing our internal biases about family roles and disrupting the stigma associated with men taking time off work to care for their children.

The internalized bias that drives men to return to work right away after the birth of a child, while negative for a variety of reasons related to fatherhood, does not negatively impact a man's career. Women, however, are in a no-win situation. Go back to work and face societal disapproval and guilt, or stay home for a while and face serious career consequences.

Meanwhile, other women may not have the means or flexibility to stay home, so they are forced back to their jobs early for the pay. New moms face a variety of different circumstances. While 12 weeks is guaranteed by the federal government, for some the entire period is paid by their employers—but for many, it is not. In small companies, women leaders often can't take off the time anyway, as they are integral to the business. Some women may feel a desire or pressure to stay home for longer than three months after having a child. In many cases, of course, they're economically unable to do so—at least without a considerable amount of belt-tightening. Factor in expensive daycare costs that take a huge portion of the family income, and the decision is even more fraught.

Regardless of how women return to work, many mothers judge themselves, riddled with guilt for not being home to nurture their children—and potentially missing the first word or the first step, or risking that the daycare worker can calm your child better than you can. Men rarely face that judgment from others or themselves.

I was lucky that I had a choice, given my own consulting practice and a very supportive husband. Even though Chip went back to work full-time, he always agreed to whatever plan I concocted that worked for me. Work full-time and have childcare? Work part-time and spend dedicated days with the kids? I never felt my career was compromised, but I continued to struggle with my internal bias. I wanted to do it all—and do it well.

It took a good decade and three children for me to learn that something had to give. I couldn't be "all in" leading the school fundraiser *and* traveling overseas for my consulting work. I couldn't volunteer regularly in the classroom or match the creative and elaborate kids' birthday parties I saw in my community. I couldn't make it to every sporting event, dance recital, or school play.

I did my best, as all other moms do. It has all worked out well, with a strong marriage, a great career, and kids who are making their way in the world. I do wonder, though: If I knew then what I know now, would I have had a different conversation with Chip instead of letting our biases play out without intentional conversations to surface them?

It's easier to pause now, in retrospect, and question whether I did the right thing, but it's all been part of my own growth as a mother, a partner, and a leader. I understood how much identity he received from his career, and I also felt satisfied in mine. I wasn't limiting myself by choosing to stay in a more flexible job as an independent consultant. Instead, I made a careful choice and fully accepted the trade-offs. Understanding your internal bias comes with the understanding that you have a choice. If the assumption, conclusion, or belief no longer serves you, then you can shift.

ACT NOW
How to Overcome Internal Bias

1. Reflect on the biases you currently have about yourself. Are they any of these? Are there others?

   ※ "I have to be nice to be accepted."

   ※ "I need to smile more, or people will think I am mad all the time."

   ※ "I need to be firm but not abrasive to get what I want."

   ※ "I can have it all (or do it all)."

   ※ "If I want it done right, I have to do it myself."

   ※ "I shouldn't show emotion if I want to be taken seriously."

   ※ "I can't show any weakness, only perfection, if I want to succeed."

   ※ "I have to work twice as hard to get the same as 'them.'"

2. Consider how these beliefs are holding you back. What limitations are they creating? How can you change your thinking?

3. Have conversations that help you and those around you challenge any self-limiting assumptions that are preventing you or them from career advancement. Use the Ladder of Inference as a tool to surface your beliefs and better understand the beliefs of others.

4. Reducing your own bias starts with curiosity. Try a Q-storm, which focuses on asking questions rather than answering them to ensure you can fully explore the topic and eliminate bias. Invite others with different backgrounds to help generate the most useful list of questions.

   For example, a topic might be: Why haven't I been promoted in the last three years?

   Questions include:

   ※ What are my criteria for applying for a promotion?

   ※ Why do I think travel is a problem?

* What role do I aspire to?
* How often do I ask for help?
* Who could help me see a different perspective?
* Do the right people know I want to be promoted?
* Who is my sponsor?
* What could I say no to in order to free up time to focus on this next move?

Once you have listed your questions, rate them in the order that you think will uncover the root cause of your issue, focusing on the questions you haven't considered before. Then dig into answering your top three. You will likely discover something new, and in addition to helping you recognize biases, this exercise can help bring clarity about what actions to take.

While we are all well served to overcome our own internal biases, women have a higher hill to climb in the professional world, and we need to realize when we are getting in our own way. There are women we coach who won't consider a job that requires travel because of their family obligations, but they also don't even stop to discuss it with their partner because of the assumed roles in the house.

Going back to Magic Johnson, he didn't question his right to make an ask, his right to be in the room, or his right to succeed. He expected it. As women, we can learn from him. Our biases need to be checked continuously, as they will surface again and again until we intentionally work to remove the cognitive shortcut.

Let's go back to our example in the Ladder of Inference. What would happen if we started by selecting different data and making different assumptions?

The
Ladder of Inference

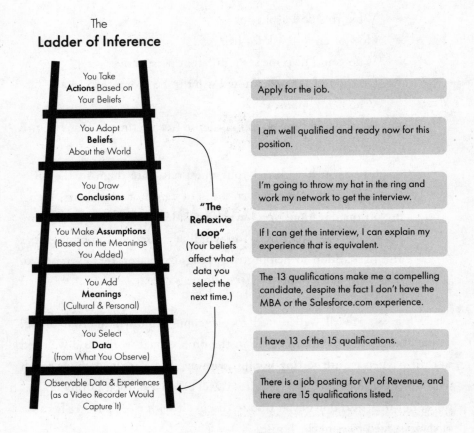

It's difficult to overcome your own negative internal biases when your external environment shaped them early in your life. It's like trying to stand tall in the ocean when wave after wave pushes you off balance and knocks you over. It will take powerful women, along with their male allies, standing together to change the flow of the current. Mostly, it will require us all to challenge these deeply ingrained beliefs and talk about them openly, in our homes and our workplaces, for us to shift our own thinking.

5

Clarity—Create Intention About Your Future

In day-to-day work as a leader, I . . .					
Project a compelling future vision for who I want to be as a leader and/or how I want to contribute in the working world.					
Rarely Demonstrate 1	Sometimes Demonstrate 2	Often Demonstrate 3	Very Often Demonstrate 4	Almost Always Demonstrate 5	N/A
O	O	O	O	O	O

Have you ever felt lost in your career, deeply aware that you're not satisfied with where you are yet just as deeply perplexed about what *would* make you happy? Have you been faced with a career decision and felt paralyzed by whether to take a new job or role? Or worse, have you jumped too soon at a new role or company because it was the easier decision or because someone told you it was the right move?

I have.

In 2017, I left two large corporate jobs—one because our company was bought, and another because a shake-up at the top meant the job that I had just been hired for no longer existed. It was a painful period of change that prompted me to take a self-defined eight-month sabbatical, my first significant pause after more than 20 years of working in the leadership industry. I knew if I didn't take this time of reflection, I would risk a reactive move into another role like the ones I had just left at two publicly traded companies.

So, I forced myself to slow down, putting a simple guiding principle in place that I'd recommend to anyone seeking a new job: each day, I committed to doing one thing for my body, one thing for my spirit, and one thing for my job search. I chose this approach because clarity is hard to obtain without the right conditions: plenty of sleep, healthy food, physical movement, and connection with others. Balancing all of those things was difficult when I was working and parenting full-time in my corporate roles, but the idea to pursue wellness on each of these levels emerged for me as I entered this time without employment and wasn't sure what to do with myself.

The days were uncomfortable at first, as I had to come to terms with some of my own limiting beliefs. Was it "wasting time" when, during the workweek, I had long coffee dates with friends or met with my Visionista group to dream about my future aspirations? Did my identity shift when I joined a tennis team and the women, whom I knew only on the courts, had little idea of my decades on the corporate fast track? Did my kids experience me differently when I suddenly had much more time to fully engage in the school rhythms and join my youngest son on the 10-minute bike ride to and from the elementary school steps, stopping at the top of the hill to share a drink from his water bottle? If the day ended and I had only sent one email or had one phone conversation to secure my next job, was that enough to count as my "one thing for my job search?" For the first time, I realized how uncomfortable it was for me to not be "doing" all the time.

Slowly, over weeks and then months, the days became completely invigorating as I allowed myself the gift of exploration, connection, and focus. I wrote often in my journal, connected with friends, and reached out to my professional network.

I will tell you in a bit how this all ended up. Right now, it's important to acknowledge that we all get lost from time to time, but when we confuse what we want with what we think we should do—or with what others want for us—we can end up discontent or even deeply unhappy until we find our way again. Working through uncertainty and gaining clarity is one of the most important challenges women face. But once clarity emerges, it acts as an incredible propeller, helping women overcome every one of the subsequent hurdles we will discuss in this book.

WHAT IS CLARITY, EXACTLY?

Clarity is a deep sense of knowing who you are—your calling, your values, your dreams—and how you want to activate that in the world. It is a guidepost that changes with self-awareness and life evolution, and it helps us make daily choices about how and where to focus our time and energy. It allows us to attract what we want most in our life and say no to the things that don't align with helping us achieve that. With clarity, we can create the life and career we want; without it, life happens *to* us.

WHY IS THIS A HURDLE FOR WOMEN?

Since we began gathering data in 2016 on the hurdles to women's advancement, clarity has consistently surfaced as one of the top three hurdles. Why is that? One hypothesis is that, over time, women have been socialized to meet the needs of others and not encouraged to focus on themselves. We naturally nurture, support, and coach others—from friends and partners to children and staff. With so much giving, it's easy to place our attention externally and inadvertently fail to create the intention or space for our own clarity to emerge.

After working with women of all ages over decades on creating their life visions, or even short-term aspirations like their next jobs, these are the most common responses I hear when I ask them what success looks like a few years into the future:

"I've never thought about it."

"I don't know what I want."

"I don't know how to find clarity."

"What if you declare what you want and then don't get it—isn't that worse than not identifying what you want at all?"

Maybe we have such uncertainty about the future because we're too busy focusing on others, or it feels like too much of a risk to dream of the life we want and then fail to create it, or we are just too busy to prioritize it. But we know that men tend to know what they want for their career and go for the next job, even when they don't meet all the qualifications. They are much more likely to focus on themselves and their career goals without guilt or hesitation. Conversely, when women are asked what we aspire to, we gravitate toward roles that help *others* excel, like coaching or mentoring team members.

To be clear, the business world needs our natural strengths and propensity to nurture, collaborate, and support. But we can also learn from the men in our lives and unapologetically declare our aspirations for ourselves, with us at the center of those aspirations, as opposed to describing our success through the lens of how it will benefit others.

WHAT HAS CHANGED IN THE LAST FEW YEARS?

By mid-2021, the Great Resignation was in full swing, fueled by women who saw the opportunity to make a change as we reassessed our lives during the COVID-19 pandemic. My concern is that many women may have left to get away from what they *don't* want—stress, commute, longer hours, etc.—and the result of this reactive orientation will keep them from fulfilling their deeper potential. My hope is that these moves—either to new jobs, reduced hours, hybrid or remote work, or leaving the workforce altogether—aligned to their aspirations for their lives and for their careers. That's the result of clarity, and having it draws us closer to our highest aspirations.

Let's look at a few examples from my own life that illustrate the power of clarity.

CLARITY IN REAL LIFE

My Visionista group was an essential resource during my eight-month sabbatical. I'd recommend a support structure like this to everyone, as gaining clarity is best achieved by working with others. They are the family you choose, not necessarily the one you are born into, because they will cheer for you, challenge you, and pick you up when you're broken. While I've had many variations of this type of support in my life, my current visioning group is a small set of women who came together 15 years ago when our kids were starting elementary school. We've been together through every parenting and life phase, and now our children are mostly adults. These women are my people—the ones who have the same deep interest and desire to create their best lives and to support me in creating mine.

In late 2017, we agreed to dedicate a few months to meeting weekly and working our way through a book called *Designing Your Life*, written by Bill Burnett and Dave Evans. The authors are Silicon Valley innovators and Stanford University educators who apply design principles to life design. This book gave me just the process and collaboration I needed to pause, get curious, and examine my entire career. I determined what kinds of colleagues, teams, and environments brought me joy versus depleting my energy. I focused on the skills and strengths I wanted most to contribute and on the kind of roles that would allow me to embrace those strengths.

From there, I created quick prototypes that propelled me into action around three potential paths forward, and I focused my daily "do one thing for my job search" activity on meeting people who could help me determine which path would bring the most opportunity and fulfillment in the next stage of my career. The three paths were very different: return to the large corporate world, where I could run a business unit; restart IntraVision, my consulting company I had shuttered eight years prior; or find a small- to middle-market company where I could have an executive role.

This time of reflection paid off. Through dozens of conversations with new and existing members of my network, I explored all three paths. Clarity didn't come to me in a specific "eureka" moment. Instead, it emerged slowly as I processed my evolving awareness with the Visionistas, my family, mentors, and advisors. It became clear to me that in my next role, I wanted to have more direct impact, more influence, and more freedom to set the vision and strategy for a company. I also wanted to inspire and engage teams to achieve aspirational goals. That meant being at the decision-making table alongside a board and other C-level executives. I could picture myself as the CEO or in a number-two role at a privately held company in the leadership training and education sector that generated up to $200 million in revenue. That focus crystallized for me that I would leave behind publicly traded companies. It also meant I would not reinstate my own consulting firm that I had paused during the Great Recession when I returned to the corporate world. Instead, I pointed my job search toward startups, nonprofit organizations, and private equity–backed companies in the leadership or human capital space. Within six months, I had real opportunities to consider across all those categories, something I could not have even imagined the prior year.

That's the power of vision and intention. Once you're clear on what you want, the universe conspires to help you achieve it. And the clearer you are, the more energy you put out into the world about that vision. Soon, people you do not even know today will emerge, and opportunities you didn't even know existed will manifest. I've seen it happen time and again with my own life and in the lives of those I care about and coach. But it's up to us to set the energy in motion, and that takes doing the hard work to create a picture of what success looks like for you, at a specific point in time, about your life—or any aspect of it. For me, at that point my focus was my career.

When I say clarity creates the energy for the universe to conspire to help you get what you want, this is what I mean: I would never have conceived of myself as a private equity–backed CEO when I left the publicly traded companies in 2017. In fact, I didn't truly understand at the time what private equity companies actually did—their business model, their cycle of buying and selling portfolio companies, and certainly not their talent acquisition strategy. But as I gained clarity and explained to my network exactly what I was looking for in my next role, *they* got excited to introduce me to their network, which led me to learn more and more about opportunities in private equity.

Within 90 days of choosing the path I would follow, a headhunter reached out to me via LinkedIn. She was the head of the private equity practice from one of the largest search firms in the world and was calling to see if I was interested in the CEO role at Linkage, Inc., a company I hadn't heard of previously. After some preliminary internet research and a few phone calls, I was excited to explore the opportunity. Within a few weeks, I received the job offer; within two months, I started the new role; and I'm now in the fifth year of the best job I've ever had.

There are a few important things to note when it comes to clarity. First, if you do not have a clear view of the path you want to be traveling, it is better to slow down than rush ahead reactively at the first opportunity that comes your way. It would have been a grave mistake if I had taken the easier path and joined another large company, where I could have run another business unit but still not have been at the executive table. Second, if you aren't yet sure of what you want and can't articulate it to others, share what you do know—the skills you want to use or passion you want to pursue or work environment you desire. Talk to others about how they gained clarity and what they did to pursue their vision. When people approach me for career advice, it is always so much easier—and more satisfying—to guide and support them if they have a clear idea of what they want.

SEEK CLARITY AT EVERY AGE AND STAGE

While the story I just shared took place in recent years, age and experience aren't required to create clarity. Younger women can and should make it a practice to seek clarity early on. If not, it's too easy to get "stuck" in the same type of job that we sought (or perhaps drifted into) as a young professional. Inertia can set in and, before we realize it, decades go by with no real progress toward creating the reality we really want. There are specific moments in every decade in my life when gaining clarity instigated significant life changes.

I wasn't yet 30 when I began to feel uneasy with my chosen career. I'd worked for three different companies in increasingly prestigious public relations roles for nearly seven years on three continents. I had the ultimate job I had aspired to when I completed graduate school. But deep down, while I appreciated the field—and was good at it—I knew it was not my destiny. The job wasn't helping me fulfill my purpose, but I wasn't clear on what was missing.

At that point I decided I would go back to school and get my MBA to figure it out. I studied for the GMAT, applied to Emory's executive MBA program, and was accepted. As I reviewed the course syllabus, my heart sank. The required classes in accounting, finance, and statistics would be soul-sucking, and I couldn't answer the simple question: "What will an MBA get you?" Before spending money I didn't have on what I feared could be a big mistake, I decided to defer for a year and work on getting clarity.

I scoured the landscape at Coca-Cola and used my relationships to conduct research. I had good friends and colleagues in public affairs, marketing, HR, operations, and customer support. I also asked for time with select business unit executives—all men at the time—because I was curious about how they rose up the ranks. My role in public relations gave me an insider's view into the executive world because we interacted with the highest levels of the firm to draft communications plans, press releases, and media responses. Throughout those early career years, I often wished I could be the one in front of the camera giving the speeches or making the statements, instead of behind the scenes writing them. Clear and evocative communication was one of my strengths, but I didn't have the chance to use it in that role.

That same year, I was privileged to work with a newly formed group at Coca-Cola called the Learning Consortium. Put in place by the late chairman Roberto Goizueta, the group was formed under a new chief learning officer in the late 1990s. The purpose of this innovation, according to Goizueta, was to create the next competitive advantage for Coca-Cola globally—to ensure the company learned faster and shared knowledge more effectively than our rivals did. To help lift this new organization, the company hired consultants with backgrounds in organizational effectiveness, leadership development, learning design, facilitation, and coaching.

This emerging field of human capital consulting was a new frontier, and I hadn't known this industry even existed. I was fascinated by the promise of working with leaders, teams, and organizations to make them better. I learned from the Consortium consultants for a year as they helped our communications function in Europe come together as a more cohesive unit. We worked on topics like team effectiveness, mental models, systems thinking, personal mastery, and executive coaching. This work stirred a passion in me that I couldn't explain, but I knew I wanted more of it. Everyone I met in that group inspired me, and the work they did enthralled me.

When the Learning Consortium leaders realized they needed more people to create a greater impact, they solicited select employees from across the business to apply for an intense nine-month training program. And that's when clarity emerged for me. Instead of paying out of my own pocket for an MBA, I asked my boss, Rob, if he would sponsor me for the program so I could serve the communications function in a different capacity as an internal consultant.

The program transformed my life, but just as I was beginning to apply my new skills, Roberto Goizueta suddenly died. He was replaced over the next few years by two CEOs in succession, the last of whom didn't believe in the significant investment of keeping high-cost consultants as full-time employees. The Learning Consortium was shut down, and the entire staff lost their jobs. My original role back in the public relations department was secure, but I now faced a bigger problem: I knew deep down I no longer wanted that role.

I was distraught—just as I had gained clarity, my opportunity was taken away. I approached Craig Cohon and Michael Chavez, two respected colleagues in the Consortium, who gave me sound advice: "Just sit with the discomfort. Hold your aspiration with your current reality. The tension will resolve itself, and opportunity will unfold with time. Your clarity has already created the energy needed."

Within six months, I left Coca-Cola and jumped at the chance to go to an internet startup that needed a director of communications. I liked the idea of building a business, but after a year I was even more certain that I did not want another communications job. I needed that opportunity, however, to give me the confidence to start my own leadership consultancy, called IntraVision. Coca-Cola became my first client, so I picked right back up where I had left off, doing the work I loved but making three times more than I did as a full-time employee. I spent the next eight years honing my consulting skills and engaging in incredible projects globally alongside the very people who had lost their jobs at Coca-Cola, who I respected deeply. IntraVision also gave me the flexibility I wanted when I had children—to work from home four days a week and dedicate Fridays to caring for them.

I have come to understand the incredible power of clarity and have practiced gaining it across the course of my life, with a special emphasis on my career. Clarity is never fixed, as conditions in your current reality change constantly—a company reorganization, the birth of a child, a global pandemic! Any significant change creates the impetus to answer the question "Is what I said I wanted still what I really want? If not, how has my clarity shifted?" There is power in putting structures in place to reflect and create the clarity for what you most want in your life—annually, quarterly, and especially in important moments of transition or opportunity. Write your vision down, share it with others, and continue to test and evolve it. In short, you need to own it.

Here are a few exercises to help you.

ACT NOW
How to Gain Clarity

There is no perfect way to gain clarity, but it does require dreaming, which is best done with time and space to play, whatever that looks like for you. It may include writing, drawing, or finding pictures in magazines that inspire you. It certainly helps to have your own version of a Visionista group. And it often doesn't happen in a constrained period. The capability for vision is like any other muscle—the more you use it, the faster and more effective it becomes.

1. CREATE A CLARITY STATEMENT

A clarity statement is a succinct vision of your ideal future state. It is what you will need to share with others so they can get creative with you and offer help. It takes time and energy to gain clarity, but I have found this to be one of life's most worthy investments. Sharing your vision first with people who care about you most—your family, friends, close colleagues—helps you gain even more clarity, and once you declare publicly what it is you're striving for, you are much more likely to prioritize your time to achieve it.

Your clarity statement could include these elements:

❋ Your vision for the future: What is your role? What Superpowers are you using? Is it aspirational enough? Be concrete and specific.

❋ Your values: What is important to you? What do you prioritize naturally?

❋ Your calling: What is it that makes you most excited? What do you feel "born to do"? Where do you thrive?

When writing your clarity statement, try to follow these simple guidelines. Your vision should be:

❋ Specific enough to know it when you have it

❋ Something you want, not something you don't want

❋ What you truly desire, not what you think is possible

❋ Set in the present, as if you already have it

❋ You-centric; you should see yourself in the picture

❋ Voluntary; you are not obliged to create it

❋ A result, not a process

All clarity statements are not created equal. Here are a few real examples from our work with women leaders to help you create your own clarity statement.

Example #1: Not So Good

Communicate with confidence and lead by example so our team feels genuinely supported, understood, and motivated to be future thinking.

This woman's statement is more focused on the team outcomes than on her individual goals. It's missing her aspiration for the future, and it feels too "present day"—there isn't any stretch involved. It's also not a concrete enough outcome—it is not measurable, and thus it would be too difficult to know when or if she achieves this goal.

Example #2: Getting Better

I would like to lead by example and help people grow in their thinking and capabilities. I want to cultivate a team that thrives through open communication and investment in each other. I would like my team to operate efficiently and effectively through me being a leader who is forward thinking and insightful. I want to stay healthy and lead a balanced life where I can continue to look for opportunities inside and outside the company to learn and grow.

This one focuses on how the leader wants to operate in the context of work and life. However, it uses conditional language—"I would like" and doesn't include her vision or dreams for the future. What specific position or role is she striving for? You are more likely to achieve your goals if you can share explicitly what you want and picture it in the present, as if you have it now.

Example #3: Even Better

As an executive leader, I contribute meaningfully to the advancement of women leaders and inclusive workplaces. I speak publicly on these topics and generate meaningful insights on the issues. While leading multiple teams, I am a fair and smart leader who grows others' skills, solves problems, and generates ideas while effectively balancing work, family, fun, health, and physical activity.

That is the clarity statement created by Kristen Howe, Linkage's chief product officer and my longtime colleague. I love the detail that she uses, describing her future state in the present tense as if she already has it in its entirety, even though parts of it—like becoming a regular public speaker—are still aspirational. It also includes her explicit values of helping others develop while maintaining a focus on her own health, relationships, and joy.

Once you create your clarity statement, share it with a few people and ask for input. This should be an iterative process, and others can help you understand what is clear and what needs to be refined.

What If You Are Having Trouble Writing Your Clarity Statement?

It may help to start with this broader personal visioning exercise, which I have used in coaching and workshops for many years. You can focus on just one piece of your life or create a holistic vision of what you most want as you integrate all aspects of your life into an entire picture. Write or draw whatever you see or hear or feel, and if you get frustrated, remember that clarity emerges with time, energy, and focus.

2. PERSONAL VISIONING EXERCISE

This exercise works best if you can complete it in a quiet, comfortable place, away from interruptions. A suggested process is to read through the categories and allow yourself to be creative, to daydream, and then to write down what comes into your mind.

As you proceed with this exercise, you will notice that it is about so much more than your work, which is by design. Our career is an important component in our life, but work impacts—and is impacted by—every other aspect of our lives as well, including our relationships, health, and community. If the culture of your workplace causes you to bring home your stress and anger, it will certainly impact your relationships. If your job requires you to commute long distances, it may be at odds with your desire to work from home. This exercise is a focusing mechanism for life change.

That said, it is perfectly fine to start with just one category or jump into all of them at once.

Exercise:

Imagine your life is *exactly* the way you want it to be. You are achieving the results you most deeply desire.

* **Self-image:** Picture yourself as the kind of person you most want to be. What do you look like? What do people say about you? What are you doing with your life?

* **Health:** You are totally and completely healthy: physically, spiritually, emotionally, mentally. What does optimal health look like for you? What gives you energy? What are your rituals for rest and reward?

* **Home:** Take a tour of your ideal living environment. What does it look like? What smells, sounds, people, and experiences do you find there? How do you feel in your home?

* **Relationships:** Widen your lens to the people most important to you. Picture yourself with them. Describe the qualities of the relationships you have with them. What do your ideal relationships look like? What is most important about those relationships?

* **Work:** Shift your focus now to your work. Imagine it is an environment where you are at your best. It is fulfilling and fun; you are doing the work that is most meaningful for you. You are recognized for your work, and you are deeply satisfied with the results you create. Describe what you see. What talents and abilities do you use? What is the work environment that supports you doing your best? What do your relationships look like at work?

* **Community:** Widen your lens even further to your ideal community (whatever community means for you—work, where you live, your spiritual community, etc.). What does that look like? What is your contribution to your community?

* **Special interests and hobbies:** Picture yourself doing whatever you enjoy for leisure and fun. What interests and activities bring you joy? How do you express your passion for life? What are you learning?

* **Life purpose:** Imagine your life has a unique purpose—fulfilled through your work, your relationships, and the way you live. You are living that unique purpose every day. What is your purpose?

Scan back through what you've written in response to these prompts, and add or delete anything as you get clearer. If there is someone you feel close to and can share this with, do so. It helps bring your vision to life!

A great thing about life is that clarity continues to evolve as we live and learn. It's okay to change our minds, shift our priorities, and choose new paths. Every experience is part of our learning, and it's better to make our choices boldly and consciously than to drift along and let life happen to us.

All of this means we will need to use our clarity skills again and again. Start practicing them now. The sooner you master the art of gaining clarity—and making changes based on what you discover about yourself— the sooner you'll be able to shape a rich and meaningful life you love.

Proving Your Value—Stop Doing So Much

RATE YOURSELF (1–5)

In day-to-day work as a leader, I . . .					
Spend more time engaging, inspiring, and enabling others than trying to do it all myself.					
Rarely Demonstrate 1	Sometimes Demonstrate 2	Often Demonstrate 3	Very Often Demonstrate 4	Almost Always Demonstrate 5	N/A
○	○	○	○	○	○

"Work smarter, not harder."

For most of my life I hated this saying, as I never understood how to act on it. I knew it was about prioritizing and delegating, but both meant letting go of responsibilities and tasks—and I was never convinced I could let go of anything. All the work I was doing at the office and at home seemed critically important. The hours I've clocked for most of my life have been extreme, and "hard worker" has been part of my identity for as long as I can remember. For decades, I wore it as a badge of honor, and the need to flash this badge still plagues me at times.

I'm not the only one who feels this way. Out of all the hurdles that Linkage has identified, measured, and developed across nearly 120,000 women and their raters who have taken our assessment, Proving Your Value is the one that stands out as the highest hurdle, the one that represents the greatest challenge for women. *Every. Single. Year.*

Why? Most women try to do it all, by ourselves, perfectly. This tendency impacts our mental health and well-being, our feeling of balance, and, perhaps most importantly, our ability to show up at our best—at work, at home, or in the community.

How has your life been impacted by trying to do it all? Where can you begin to let go, to give up control? Have you ever considered that when you step back, it allows others to step in and demonstrate their own value?

WHAT IS PROVING YOUR VALUE, EXACTLY?

Proving Your Value stems from the mistaken belief that *if I put my head down and work harder, people will notice and acknowledge my value.* As we mentioned in chapter one, this external bias starts at home, where women, and mothers in particular, are three times more likely than fathers to be responsible for most of the housework and caregiving.[1] Called the "second shift," this includes the unpaid household labor like cleaning, food prep, and caregiving for children and other family members. We then bring that ownership of all details to the office and add the "third shift" with unpaid office work, which we'll discuss in a moment.

It can be exhausting and discouraging, especially if it's hard for us to delegate and allow room for someone to learn what we "know" how to do, or even do it their own way. The reality is that perfectionism and the desire for control prevent us from fully stepping into leadership roles. As leaders, it becomes more important as we rise to define our value less through the work we do ourselves and more through the work of others.

Much of this overwork is our own doing and stems from the mistaken idea that if it's going to get done right, "I have to do it myself"—that pesky internal bias we introduced in chapter four. Even if things really *are* better when we take charge, the unintended consequences are significant. Over time, we get angry, tired, or resentful (or maybe all three) because we're shouldering so much responsibility. And others—our family, staff, or colleagues—learn that their efforts aren't welcomed or good enough because we refuse their help. So, they stop trying so hard themselves, which in turn prevents them from opportunities to develop their own skills. It's a difficult cycle to break. The good news is that we really don't have to "prove our value" by doing everything ourselves.

By finding clarity, we can focus on those priorities in our lives that are most important to us and ensure we allocate our energy to those. If we can release control and the expectation of doing everything ourselves, we can spend more time engaging, inspiring, and enabling others to help.

WHY IS THIS A HURDLE FOR WOMEN?

Women have long been over-rowing the boat. We've traditionally taken on the role of primary caretaker, educator, and cook, but in the last 60 years we've added professional, leader, and mentor—all without relinquishing any one of our previous roles.

By the time women enter the leadership ranks, we have already spent an enormous amount of time living up to unrealistic, external standards of perfection. It may manifest as a misguided belief that we aren't "good enough," so we work harder to demonstrate our competence. We also may live and lead from fear—fear of failure, fear of being "found out" as an imposter, or fear of saying no, which may disappoint others or prevent us from being offered future opportunities.

Whatever the source of the need to prove our value, there's little doubt that we women are conditioned to lend a hand, whether at work, at home, or at the community fundraiser.

Let's be honest: most women want people to like us, and we feel a sense of obligation to demonstrate how responsible, generous, and capable we are. I've rarely seen men operate with the same sense of duty or obligation, and it befuddles me. Why do I feel guilty when I don't volunteer at the school fair, attend every work function, or answer every email, but my spouse does not? Women often conflate doing more work with providing more impact, but this is flawed thinking. The much greater impact is to empower or teach others instead of trying to do it all ourselves.

The answer to overcoming this hurdle, of course, is to stop taking on more work for yourself, while engaging and enabling others to step in and step up. But this is far easier said than done! Letting go of some work requires a difficult shift in your own mental calculation—from constantly trying to prove your value by doing *everything* to providing value by doing the *select few things* that align with your passion and your strengths (the things that you discovered in your work on Clarity). It's a shift from focusing on the *quantity* or volume of your work to the *quality* of the very specific work that only you can do or that you want to do.

To align our work with our aspirations and our strengths, we need to get more comfortable telling people where we excel and promoting our own accomplishments. If you know, for example, that you have a gift for managing a project through to execution as opposed to green-fielding new ideas, it may not be wise to volunteer for the early stage of an innovation project as opposed to proving your specific value when the project moves to the activation phase.

We'll discuss further in chapter eight on Branding & Presence whether you are building the leadership brand that aligns to your aspiration and if people know you for the qualities required to achieve it. For now, though, be aware that others likely don't know your aspiration unless you are regularly communicating your contribution or accomplishments so it's clear when and where you can add the most value. Be thoughtful about what to promote. Don't tell your boss how great you were at capturing the meeting notes or editing a document if those skills don't align with your future aspirations or how you want people to see you. The necessity to self-promote is covered further in chapter seven, on Recognized Confidence.

WHAT HAS CHANGED IN THE LAST FEW YEARS?

The reality for working women has always been the simultaneous juggle between our work and domestic lives, but two recent ignition points further upset that imbalance. The explosion of the virtual workplace in 2020 made the "second shift" much more visible, as it was no longer separated from the physical workplace in space and time. Suddenly, there was no hiding the kids or animals or parents, and many women I spoke to were relieved that they could finally stop pretending they didn't have other aspects of their life outside of work that needed attention. The reality was exposed, and it created greater understanding and empathy. Yet, the struggle and anxiety were real, with women trying to blend home and work simultaneously and "do it all" in such a visible way.

The other explosion has been the "third shift," the extra unpaid work women take on in the workplace. It has evolved from the traditional office housework like taking meeting notes or tidying the conference rooms to the more complex caring needs in the workplace around mental health and diversity, equity, and inclusion (DEI) work, especially with the rise in awareness and urgency focused on underrepresented populations.[2] The findings in the 2021 Women in the Workplace report by LeanIn.org and McKinsey & Company, the largest study on the state of women in corporate America, brought this insight to light: Compared to men at the same level, women in senior leadership are 63 percent more likely to provide emotional support to employees, 21 percent more likely to help their team navigate work/life challenges, and 17 percent more likely to ensure their teams' workloads are manageable.[3] Additionally, women leaders are twice as likely to spend a substantial amount of time doing DEI work outside of their formal job responsibilities, such as recruiting and mentoring individuals from underrepresented populations and leading employee resource groups. And at every level, women are more likely than men to show up as allies to women of color.

Think about your own team and organization: Who does most of the nurturing work, such as coaching or mentoring, or the administrative work, like note-taking and organizing office meetings? Who takes on the work no one else volunteers to do? You're likely to find it's the women in your organization who step up to take on these tasks. It's one more way we jump in to try to prove our value.

While this extra "third shift" work is critical, there is a big problem—these efforts aren't measured, recognized, or rewarded in the form of additional compensation. Instead, this work has led to additional exhaustion, with 43 percent of women experiencing burnout by the end of 2022, up from a third of women reporting burnout in 2020.[4]

So, it wasn't surprising, perhaps, that in 2021, when the COVID-19 pandemic began to lift, the Great Resignation exploded, led by the exodus of women. With colleagues leaving and jobs being reimagined, those of us who stayed picked up even more of the work.

I felt it in my own team. When three female executive team members chose to leave Linkage across six months in 2021, it was for very different reasons: the first had an excellent opportunity to return to a larger company and build a new business unit; another wanted to do more custom consulting work that we no longer offered; and the third left the corporate world altogether to start a charcuterie catering business in her home.

In retrospect, their departures were a gift, given the havoc that COVID-19 was wreaking on our business and our clients. We needed to be leaner at the top, and we had very talented professionals underneath them who had each been at Linkage for a long time and were ready to grow in their respective roles. So, we promoted three senior leaders from within and reenvisioned the organizational structure. It wasn't easy. Half the executive team was new to their roles, and all of us took on the additional work of the departing employees. With the internal disruption and external market chaos, we buckled in for a rocky ride.

There is a difference between working hard and proving your value. We all had to step up to run a business during one of the biggest crises of the last century. We worked tirelessly, but we were aligned to an aspirational vision. We collectively decided which work to prioritize for the executive team, what could be delegated, and what we needed to let go of altogether. By the end of 2021, we were depleted after two very intense years, but it was also exhilarating when we hit our goals. We kept the company alive and doubled down on our plan to continue our business transformation, accelerating our innovation through the COVID-19 period. In times like this, however, we need to ensure that we don't maintain this pattern of overwork as a "new normal" once a crisis has simmered. That is proving to be hard, given the increasing pace of change.

PROVING YOUR VALUE IN REAL LIFE

Let's use some stories to illustrate what proving your value looks like and how to overcome the inclination to prove your value by doing more. As you'll see, there are five powerful strategies: stop trying to do it all, let go of work that is not aligned to your aspiration, get more comfortable saying no, release the need to be perfect, and enlist and inspire others to do the work we can delegate.

Stop Trying to Do It All

When I started as Linkage CEO in mid-2018, I was determined to immerse myself in the role by engaging in every part of the business. I knew it was critical to accomplish some major milestones within the first 90 days. I needed to formulate a business model and strategic plan leading up to a board meeting in the fall, where we would make the case for a capital raise to support the growth and transformation of the firm across the next three years. I wanted to develop a deeper understanding and point of view on our research and data, along with our service offerings, pricing, contracting, and business management systems. I wanted to get thoughts and feedback from some of our customers and advisory board members. And overriding it all, I wanted to make a good first impression on the staff, as I knew the sudden exit of the previous CEO—timed with my simultaneous arrival—had been a shock to them.

To create transparency in my plans, I engaged the team with monthly town halls and weekly video messages, coined JVlogs (Jennifer's video blogs). Within 180 days, I had hired three new executives, and turnover at the top began. Within the year, only two of the executive team members I inherited were still with me. I had asked one person to move to a lower-level role, and he left the company instead; the others resigned because they had not chosen the transformation that I had committed to drive forward, and they either didn't want to adopt their evolving role in it or didn't believe in me personally.

In retrospect, I tried to do way too much, too fast. Instead of taking a step back and investing more time in listening and learning, I dove right in to fulfill my commitment to the board. When I told the executive team a few months into the role that I was going to "test" our Linkage 360° leadership assessment on myself and would value their honest feedback if they were willing to give it, I realized that I was not hitting the mark in some areas that were important to me. Namely, some of my team felt I was driving everything full steam ahead on my own and not engaging them enough in the process.

In other words, in trying to prove my value and do it all, I was actively disengaging the very people I needed to enlist for our transformation to succeed. As I reflected much later, it was the quality of the engagement with the executive team I was missing in my effort to solidify some "quick wins" early in my CEO tenure.

Let Go of What Is Not Aligned to Your Aspiration or What You Must Own Directly

It's easy for us to see when someone else is doing too much. It's a lot harder to practice letting go ourselves, especially when we feel compelled by perfectionism or duty. There are things we simply can't let go of given the real responsibility of our roles, whether as a professional, partner, community member, or mother. As the CEO, for example, I ultimately own the organization's vision, strategy, and resource allocation. The good news is, I am directly responsible for little else, and I've grown aware that many things are better off without my contribution or perspective.

Here is one example: Shortly after I started my job at Linkage, we moved into a beautiful new office. Kelly Gruber, our office manager, had spent months planning for the transition, all the way down to choosing the carpet and furniture. I have little expertise or interest in office decor, so when Kelly approached me to make final decisions on the wall color and artwork, I respectfully declined. Instead, we recruited a volunteer cross-functional "culture" committee and gave them a small budget to bring the space to life with all the finishing touches, from the kitchen to the conference rooms. I was overwhelmed by their passion, creativity, and output. They were energized by the opportunity to make their contributions, and I stayed out of the way.

I've tried to grow in my awareness similarly at home. As a parent, I need to ensure my children are nurtured, clothed, and fed, but I don't have to be the one to lead all those efforts. My husband is a much better shopper than I am, and while he makes more impulsive purchases than I would when at the mall with our kids, I try to be effusive in my praise for his decisions because it's one less thing for me to manage, and I appreciate his efforts. Instead of shopping, I would rather do the dog walking with any one kid and stop for a treat at the local coffee shop. I also don't like to cook after a long day in my home office, so instead of arguing about who plans menus and cooks, we simplify the process by buying meals through an online food service. It is more expensive than doing the grocery shopping and preparation ourselves, but it's an investment we're willing to make. It means I can allocate my limited "free" time to exercise, activities with my family or friends, or extra career pursuits—doing things that either I must own (my health) or that align to my aspiration (my relationship with my family, my spiritual growth, and my job).

In the "Act Now" section of this chapter, we offer you a specific framework to help with decision-making about what work you may consider releasing.

Practice Saying No

When you know what aligns with your aspiration, strengths, and direct ownership, you can start the very important practice of saying no to things that don't fit.

Deep into the COVID-19 pandemic in October 2020, I was invited by my incredible CEO coach, Jacquie Hart, to a special virtual event where dozens of other mid-market CEOs would share challenges and best practices around how they were overcoming the significant crises we faced related to growth, expenses, cash, and talent. I was trying out the network to determine if I wanted to join, and I was excited about the opportunity.

We were immersed in strategic planning for "COVID recovery" for the following year, so I joined a small breakout group focused on that topic. In the Zoom room, I saw a familiar mix that I had experienced my whole career: of the eight of us in the group, five were white men, another man appeared to be Latino, and there was one other white woman we'll call Laura. After the introductions, I realized Laura was a vendor to CEOs, so she was there to observe more than contribute. In other words, I was the lone female CEO.

The facilitator of the group was a white man, and he requested that we pick one person to capture the conversation and report back to the larger group. I didn't feel the need to volunteer as a first-time guest, so I stayed quiet. After an awkward pause, one of the men said, "I am not a good notetaker, so I volunteer Jennifer to take the notes." I quickly decided that I didn't need to prove my value as a notetaker, so I respectfully declined and cited my newbie status. I then took a deep breath because I knew what would happen next. The same man said, "Then I volunteer Laura to take the notes." She accepted the role, and I was furious.

My Inner Critic went straight One Up to judgment: *Of course a man would ask the women to do the office housework! I can't believe that even in a virtual environment, men are still using the excuse that their handwriting or administrative skills aren't as strong as women's!* Not one man, not even the facilitator, said anything, even as I willed this to be a teaching moment. The meeting proceeded, and I checked out mentally. I had practiced saying no, but another woman had stepped in to fulfill the stereotypical expectation. In retrospect, I could have shifted to Compassionate Center and become curious. I could have gently pointed out what I was seeing and asked if others saw it, too. But I didn't; I was stuck.

It happened again 18 months later, this time back in person at a business development conference filled with HR executives. We had broken into teams to do small-group work, and I had spontaneously started to take notes privately because it helps me learn and retain knowledge. The male VP of talent at a prestigious insurance company offered to do the report-out the next morning, so I gave him the notes I had taken in case they were helpful. I was shocked when he started his report-out with these words: "I'd like to give Jennifer the credit for taking good notes so I can do the report-out."

In all fairness, I don't think he meant any harm by this statement; he may have thought I would appreciate receiving credit for my efforts. However, as a CEO—a *woman* CEO—I was humiliated by being positioned publicly as "the notetaker," and felt I needed to jump into the presentation to add additional insight when he finished. In that moment, I vowed that I would talk to him privately and share with him the impact of his words, but the moment passed, and he left the conference before I could reach him.

Women, beware: if you aspire to be known for your own thoughts and not for capturing others', carefully select what you volunteer for—you may be better off reporting out the insights versus capturing them!

Release the Need for Perfection

I've seen countless women in my closest circles postpone or walk away from their goals and dreams—from launching a business to on-ramping back into the workforce after downshifting to raise their kids. They cite that they either don't feel ready or don't feel like things such as timing, preparedness, or the work product are "just right," and that feeling paralyzes them. After watching them lament over months or years, I lovingly ask whether, deep down, they really want those goals at all. If the answer is yes, then I challenge them to take the next step immediately, just to see how it feels, to test and learn, to try and fail, or to evolve their thinking altogether.

Do you hold higher standards for yourself than you expect from others? Do you obsess regularly over the small stuff, like the precise wording of an email or how you might interject a "smart" comment into the conversation? Perfectionism does not serve us well. It is often accompanied by worry and obsession, and, at its extreme, it can lead to anxiety, sleeplessness, and depression.[5]

As you reflect on how you might push away perfection and the urge to "do it all," remember: there are things that deserve your creative energy because they need to be done really well, and there are many things that don't. A 21st-century leadership skill is knowing the difference between these two things. It's time to give yourself permission to be less than perfect. Interestingly, the COVID-19 pandemic forced me to practice this because there simply wasn't time to do it all well. My colleague Kristen Howe is one of the best I know at documenting early thinking and lobbing it over the wall to others so they can make it better. She doesn't let perfectionism paralyze her, and I often hear her say, "It's good enough for now."

As for me, I tend to labor over the small stuff. The last 20 percent of any project, whether it's cleaning the kitchen or finishing a board deck, seems to consume 80 percent of the time, and I often work until the outcome meets my expectations. But what if I stopped at the 80 percent and allowed others to step in? That recognition leads to the final, and critical, recommendation for overcoming the inclination to do it all.

Enlist and Inspire Others to Do the Work So We Can Let Go

In the spring of 2022, I slapped four Post-it notes on the wall above my computer to ensure my work and energy were focused on the small set of critical priorities that aligned to my aspiration and that I uniquely owned.

The first two were newer capabilities and a stretch for me—writing this book and delivering paid keynote addresses each month. Both had been part of my bucket list for as long as I can remember, and both supported the organizational brand and business transformation we have pursued at Linkage for many years. I depended on the help and input of others on my team, but ultimately, I owned the outcomes. I couldn't delegate those tasks.

The third initiative was the evolving three-year vision and strategic plan, which would be kicked off in June with our executive team off-site and staff retreat. While it was a collaborative process, filled with financial modeling and milestones that we presented annually every October to the board of directors, it had historically been a process and document that I owned.

The final priority was selling the company, something I had committed to doing within five years of my arrival in 2018. The entire executive team was involved in this change of ownership, but my COO and I were driving the lion's share of the work. I couldn't let that go, either.

By summer, all four priorities were peaking, and I was overcommitted. I shared that feeling in the biweekly meeting with my executive team, fearing that they felt the same way. Instead, they jumped in to help. Kristen took over the documentation and evolution of the strategic plan, which was well underway but hadn't yet progressed enough to take it to the next level. Shannon Bayer agreed to lead select book chapters for which she had important experience and perspective. Sarah Breigle led the communication strategy for the company acquisition to ensure we would be ready when the announcement went public. Kristin Barrett, our head of consulting, took over some client deliveries that had been on my schedule initially, saving me several trips and a lot of preparation that didn't align to my four priorities. And I watched Rick Pumfrey, who was consumed with all the financial and legal requirements for the company sale, delegate to our external lawyer all the negotiating and contracts with an agent, publisher, editor, and the board that were required for this book. He knew he couldn't manage the work himself during this intense period, and he let it go easily.

The best part about work that summer was watching each of us on the team step up, engage, and develop through new challenges—most of which weren't comfortable—without sacrificing any of the quality of the outputs. The strategic-planning document looked different than it did when I owned it, but in many ways, Kristen improved it, and every other executive who took on pieces of what I had been trying to hold on my own improved those, too. Each time someone takes on my work and makes it better—from the office decor to the strategic plan—I slowly realize that letting go helps me and it helps them.

In my life now, with my involvement at work, at home, or in the community, I more frequently ask myself what I can let go of and how others can help. It allows me to stay focused on what only I can do, and it's fulfilling to see others achieve better outcomes than I could have on my own.

ACT NOW
How to Stop Proving Your Value

The reason Proving Your Value is the single largest hurdle women face is because it is so psychologically hard to overcome. The stories and guidance

I've just shared, and the action items coming up, are meant to build aware-ness and inspire change, no matter how small. Wherever you are in your process of letting go is right where you are supposed to be, and each moment is an opportunity to start anew. It's all part of the journey, and perhaps this five-step strategy can help:

1. **Identify your value.** It's important to understand and articu-late your unique value at work. This means getting clear on your strengths and priorities and aligning your time with them. Then you can use the matrix on the next page to diagnose and ana-lyze the work you are doing. First, open your daily calendar to see where you are spending your time.

   I hope something surprises you. We don't do enough thinking about where we want to spend our time versus where we actually do. We get caught up in all the activity and busyness, especially given the societal premium placed on having a completely full schedule. If you are too busy, it's probably because you are saying yes more than you need to.

   Based on your calendar, analyze the last month of your sched-ule. As you look at your tasks and meetings, create a list of how you bring unique value to those meetings. Your list may consist of things like your critical perspectives, your skill sets, and your rela-tionships. You may find you aren't bringing unique value to every task and meeting, so note that, too.

2. **Diagnose your work.** Once anchored in how you bring value, you can decipher what you will choose to do to the very best of your ability—and what work you can hand off or stop doing alto-gether. Note that this applies equally to your "second shift" of unpaid labor at home and "third shift" of unpaid office work!

   Categorize the work that you do today into four segments:

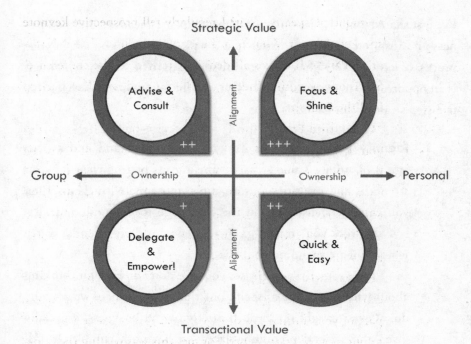

* **"Advise and Consult."** This is work you don't own but help others with, likely your direct reports or peers who may want your input but not your ownership. Here you may need to let go of expectations of how work should get done and allow others to drive while you support from the sidelines. I consult with my direct reports about products, pricing, sales, and consulting goals, but I let them know that they have ultimate ownership over the process and outcome. The new shift for me was the strategic-planning process and document. While I thought I had to own it like I had previously for four consecutive years, I eventually realized I could play an advisory role.

* **"Delegate and Empower."** This is work you can completely let go of, especially if it isn't necessary or valuable for you to be in charge of it. Would it be more valuable for someone else to do it, either so they get the experience or because they bring

a unique perspective to it? I regularly tell prospective keynote speakers for our Women in Leadership Institute™ that Katharine Panessidi makes all decisions related to the conference. She is our executive director and better qualified than I am to lead those efforts.

* **"Quick and Easy."** This is work you are doing that is part of your job but not aligned with your clarity statement. Can you do it without overdoing it? What would be considered "good enough" without getting bogged down by perfectionism? All administrative work and social media falls here for me, and whatever I can't delegate, I try to complete as quickly as possible around my critical priorities.

* **"Focus and Shine."** This is work you do that aligns with your clarity and value—it's where you excel. It is yours to own as a part of your formal job or objectives. This is where you want to put most of your energy. For me, this was writing the book, delivering the keynotes, and managing the sale of the company.

3. **Prioritize and communicate your priorities**. This matrix is a fantastic way to identify what you are leading right now that you can delegate to others or stop doing altogether. It is also a communications tool to help you be transparent with your boss, direct reports, and colleagues about the work you are doing and the work you want to be doing instead. When I offered up my four critical priorities, I engaged my team in how they could help, and we all benefited.

4. **Organize your energy.** Once you know which segments your work falls into, organize your day around them. When you have the most energy, engage in the most critical things from your "Focus and Shine" bucket. For me, writing and rehearsing for keynotes are best in the quiet hours of the morning, while staff update meetings don't require a lot of preparation for me and fall under "Quick and Easy" tasks that can be scheduled for later in the day.

5. **Resist saying yes (and practice saying no).** Before agreeing to additional work, refer to this matrix and determine where that work falls. Communicate openly with your boss and ask for help in making trade-off decisions. We can demonstrate our value without losing ourselves, or our time, in the process.

For my entire life, I have been filled with ambition and worked hard to achieve at every stage. I was never fully satisfied with my results, and I've come to realize over many decades that perhaps I worked too hard.

I honor my experience and choices then, but now I want to spend more time gaining clarity about my aspirations and unique value. I want to engage, inspire, and develop others to do the same. I want to leverage my network for help. Perhaps that's what "work smarter, not harder" really means.

My dear friend Simmons Lettre shared with me this touching poem by Octavia Raheem from her book *Gather*. It spoke to me profoundly about how to (finally) overcome this hurdle, and I will leave it with you.

Invite in More Ease
by Octavia Raheem[6]

What would it mean to approach even the hardest tasks with a spirit of ease?

What if we could trust more of our essence (who + whose we are) to support our greatest endeavors?

What if we pushed less? Could we create more? Could we become greater? Can we get a seat at the table if we work with more ease? If we make it to the proverbial table, can ease have a seat with us? What outdated belief system does straining support?

I am not suggesting that we dismiss our responsibilities.

Or that we don't respond or show up. That we don't get that 5:30 a.m. practice or workout in tomorrow. I am not suggesting that we call the whole thing off. That we completely shut down, even though sometimes that's what's required.

I am actually suggesting that we become more responsible, show up fuller. That we engage in a more complete way.

Pushing, pulling, straining, grasping, huffing, puffing, dreading, avoiding, distracting, but still managing to "get it all done" perpetuates more of itself. It's a self-sustaining, yet inefficient, and tiring cycle.

If you have a mountain of work in front of you, breathe and pause. Drink water. Meditate.

Face the mountain, clearly. Can you move through the mountain AND touch the grace of ease?

Looming deadlines? Drink some tea. Play your favorite song. Dance. Then give life to that deadline. Can you inspire a spark of ease in your process?

I've made an interesting turn in my journey. I can see backward and forward. I see how the energy, attitude, relentlessness in my grind is what got me where I am.

It. Has. All. Served. Me. Well.

And it is also not sustainable. To be clear, the discipline, the ethic, the responsiveness, is absolutely sustaining. My approach is not.

I am not looking for easy ways. I am inviting more ease into my work—more trust in my Essence—the qualities that make me, me.

I am open to a place to lean more softly into the challenging, hard, and necessary prickly places of growth. Making friends with ease is a new relationship, and I can't resist the possibility it holds after a lifetime of grinding.

Are you friends with ease?

7

Recognized Confidence—Embrace Your Wisdom, Strength, and Power

RATE YOURSELF (1–5)

In day-to-day work as a leader, I . . .					
Recognize the value I bring to the organization.					
Rarely Demonstrate 1	Sometimes Demonstrate 2	Often Demonstrate 3	Very Often Demonstrate 4	Almost Always Demonstrate 5	N/A
○	○	○	○	○	○

My daughter, Madeleine, called me, distraught, after her first week at the McIntire undergraduate business school at the University of Virginia. She had made an innocent mistake when answering one of her professor's questions in front of her new classmates, the ones she would be with all year. Her perception was that the professor had criticized her response and embarrassed her in front of the class. Her confidence had been shattered, and she'd shut down for the rest of the week, replaying the scene repeatedly in her head and with others.

I don't remember exactly what I said, but I hope it sounded like this: "That sounds hard. We all have regrets from time to time about what we've said or done. But you took the risk and put yourself out there, and even if you feel you failed, you have another opportunity to try again. You'll build your confidence with increased practice, as you've done before in other situations. I know you can do it." I'm pretty sure she didn't believe me. Confidence is situational, and it can be elusive, especially for women.

There have been entire books written about confidence, with significant focus on "imposter syndrome," a phenomenon first discovered in the 1970s that disproportionately impacts women and minorities.[1] Imposter syndrome arises from self-doubt and worry that you have not earned your success, resulting in a concern that you will be "found out" and perceived as a fraud or unworthy. An expert on the topic is my friend Ruth Gotian, assistant professor of education at Weill Cornell Medicine and author of *The Success Factor*. In an excellent article in *Psychology Today*, she says that "up to 70 percent of the workforce suffers from imposter syndrome, including former First Lady Michelle Obama . . . [former] Facebook COO Sheryl Sandberg, Supreme Court Justice Sonia Sotomayor, and tennis great Serena Williams."[2]

With that group as a comparator set, it is not surprising that all women I know, even those at the highest levels of leadership, have admitted that at some point they don't feel worthy of their position or accomplishments despite overwhelming evidence of their competence. These women incorrectly attribute their success to luck or to the notion that they have somehow tricked others into thinking they are better than they perceive themselves to be. It's what my daughter was experiencing as she sat in that classroom, anxious and embarrassed.

These feelings of insecurity and self-doubt are normal and usually result from being in a new environment or unfamiliar situation. Most of us inadvertently allow our imposter syndrome to diminish our confidence, at least in the short term, but Dr. Gotian offers a surprising and optimistic perspective. She says that we can interpret imposter syndrome as well-earned—and celebrate it—as it often accompanies an achievement, like a new role, promotion, or award:

> What if we looked at imposter syndrome from a different angle? Instead of viewing it as a trigger for insecurity, anxiety, and inadequacies, what if you get imposter syndrome because you care and are motivated to succeed? What if this feeling was intertwined with your laser-focused mission to improve and advance in your career? If you are feeling imposter syndrome, it is not because you are a fraud. It is because you are putting in the time and effort, and someone is finally paying attention. . . . Your feeling of imposter syndrome is a celebration of your achievement, not a concession of your inadequacies.[3]

I love that reframing. When those imposter feelings reemerge, we can use this awareness to shift to Compassionate Center and reconsider our own internal bias about our competence, readiness, or worthiness.

If you are wondering about the difference between confidence and worthiness, it's this: Confidence is the belief that you can do things well. Worthiness is the favorable opinion (or lack thereof) of yourself—it's the quality of feeling "good enough" or deserving of attention or respect. Imposter syndrome is tied to worthiness, but it is a reinforcing loop. If we or others don't believe that our success is deserved or has been legitimately achieved by our own efforts or skills, it will impact the confidence that we have in ourselves and that others have in us.

WHAT IS RECOGNIZED CONFIDENCE, EXACTLY?

While being confident and feeling worthy are ultimately what we want, the intentional focus of this chapter is what we call *Recognized Confidence*, which entails believing in your own value in a way that shows up authentically as confidence that others also recognize and believe. To advance as women, it is important that others perceive your greatness and see your accomplishments. When they do, you'll be more likely to close the deal, secure the partnership, or get the next job. We have a lot of influence over how we demonstrate confidence.

It's also important to articulate what Recognized Confidence is *not*. A dreaded phrase I've heard throughout my professional career as an antidote to imposter syndrome or a lack of confidence is: "Fake it 'til you make it." That advice serves only to reinforce my feelings of doubt or unworthiness because when I'm actively faking confidence, I'm admitting that I don't yet believe in my value.

In 2021, Linkage honored Carla Harris with our Legend in Leadership Award. She is an author, speaker, gospel singer, mother, and senior client advisor at Morgan Stanley. I asked her on the main stage how challenging it was to be the "only" in so many rooms—the only woman, the only person of color, the only woman of color—and what she thought about the "fake it 'til you make it" approach. She said, "Every time someone says that, I cringe. I don't believe in faking it. Having trepidation and fear can be real. Don't fake it—the idea of faking something is in direct contrast to authenticity."

I've heard Carla speak many times, and her mantra is, "Your authenticity is your distinct competitive advantage." She continued to share her thoughts on the topic: "Authenticity is at the heart of inspiring everyone. If you fake it once, and then again and again, you lose the essence of who you are, and that is your competitive edge." We will discuss authenticity at length in the next chapter when we cover our leadership brand and presence.

The obvious question, then, is: What do we do if we genuinely *don't* feel confident, if we *do* feel like an imposter, even if we're really prepared? This is where we can become aware of our Inner Critic (*I'll never be ready; I'm doomed to fail*) and examine our internal bias (*Is this a story I'm telling myself that no longer serves me?*). It's time to come back to Compassionate Center and give yourself some grace.

Yes, the feeling is real. But dig deep and try to shift your beliefs. Are you in the room? Then you have earned your way into the room. Are you at the table? Then you deserve a seat at the table. You already have a track record of accomplishment, so what are you questioning, really?

Carla said one more thing that stuck with me: "No one will give you an opportunity while simultaneously hoping or expecting to see you fail. If somebody is spending their currency on you, it reflects on them. If they bet on you, they know you can do it. Sometimes, if you are lagging in your own confidence and your own courage, hold on to theirs until you catch up. They already believe it because they have spent the currency on you."

WHY IS RECOGNIZED CONFIDENCE
A HURDLE FOR WOMEN?

Recognized confidence requires self-promotion and risk-taking, two things men excel at more naturally. According to recent research by Christine Exley at Harvard Business School and Judd Kessler at Wharton,[4] there is a large gender gap in self-promotion that emerges as early as sixth grade. In their experiment, the authors gave participants an aptitude test and then asked equally performing women and men—who did not yet know their own scores—to describe their ability and performance to potential employers. They were told that their answers to the self-promotion question would be the only thing that these employers would consider when deciding who would be hired and what they would be paid. Overwhelmingly, women subjectively evaluated their own performance less favorably than men did, ranking themselves one-third lower than men ranked themselves, even though they were closer to the truth than the men, who consistently overrated their own performance. Interestingly, even when women were given their actual scores relative to others, they were still much more likely to report lower performance than men were, despite being fully aware that they had performed similarly to the men. Finally, the researchers took away all incentives to self-promote, telling participants that their answers to the questions about how well they thought they performed would not be shared with potential employers. The gender gap still persisted.

This aversion to talking about themselves or their accomplishments was confirmed in a survey named The Self-Promotion Gap,[5] which explored women's reticence of self-promotion. While the majority of women, according to the survey, avoid talking about their strengths and accomplishments, interesting differences do exist, depending on factors like race, age, and parental status. For example, the survey cites that "African American (44 percent) and Hispanic (47 percent) women are far less likely to downplay their strengths and abilities than white (60 percent) women." In our Advancing Women Leaders 360° assessment, we also find that Black and Latina women rate themselves slightly higher on Recognized Confidence, and this is also true of the ratings that others (their bosses, peers, and direct reports) give them. They can serve as good examples for other women.

Here's what I find most disheartening in the Self-Promotion Gap study: "Not only do women avoid self-promotion—*they would rather downplay their accomplishments than own up to them*. . . . seven in 10 (69 percent) women would rather minimize their successes than tell people about them." That said, a majority (83 percent) have been inspired by hearing other women talk about their successes. It's counterintuitive—we like to hear about other women's successes (much more so than men's), but at the same time, we are more comfortable making ourselves seem like less than we are. Why is that?

Perhaps it isn't surprising, given the external bias we've already covered: When women engage in assertive behavior, it tends to backfire, leading them to downplay their contributions. And women have been taught over generations the value and expectation of humility, along with the negative perception of boasting or taking credit.

However, women *can* embrace a more even balance between displaying confidence and practicing humility, just as organizations can help overcome the biases that are preventing women from demonstrating their confidence—like increasing the visibility of women's accomplishments through spotlighting promotions, access to stretch experiences, and sponsorship.

Remember that truth we learned in chapter three to help us overcome our Inner Critic: what you think and feel drives what you say and do. In promoting our accomplishments or taking on new roles, we don't need to necessarily feel confidence in ourselves, just confidence in the actions we're taking—which over time will lead to more confidence in ourselves.

WHAT HAS CHANGED IN THE LAST FEW YEARS?

Despite the perennially disappointing number of women at all levels of leadership, there are finally many more visible role models and stories that highlight them. This acknowledgment surged to the forefront in 2020 when Kamala Harris became the first woman and first woman of color elected vice president of the United States. At the same time, countries with women in power were hailed as faring the best during the height of the COVID-19 pandemic, like New Zealand, Finland, Denmark, Taiwan, and Germany.[6]

The increased focus on International Women's Day each year on March 8 is another example of global recognition and celebration of women's and girls' achievements. Many more of our clients and partners are using that day and month to raise awareness of both the progress made toward achieving gender equality and the work that remains.

In her 2013 book, *Lean In,* Sheryl Sandberg encouraged women to assert themselves at work and at home. It was a bold missive that readers and critics met with mixed reviews. Perhaps it was ahead of its time. When the #MeToo movement raised awareness of sexual assault and harassment in 2017, there was also some backlash about the credibility of the women who shared their stories. Yet, these setbacks aside, there's been a sea change in our culture over the past decade. It simply *feels* different now, with inappropriate or illegal behavior no longer tolerated and women's accomplishments and aspirations being more openly honored and supported.

RECOGNIZED CONFIDENCE IN REAL LIFE

We can't always control our feelings, but we can control our actions. The following stories are designed to give you concrete ideas about what to do to ensure others see your greatness and recognize your competence. Through your actions, your feelings of confidence will grow, and you will squelch your imposter syndrome.

Overcome Fear of Failure by Trying New Things

Recognized confidence builds when you first identify your own accomplishments. This, of course, requires taking risks to do something new, ideally something aligned with your clarity statement.

After my summer in Barcelona working as a translator and intern at the Olympic Games, I wasn't thinking about pursuing opportunities that were aligned with my purpose as much as just getting a paying job in the public relations field. I set my sights on a full-time job with Coca-Cola in Atlanta, but they dashed my dreams by informing me they didn't hire anyone without industry work experience. Instead, they offered to open the door to their public relations agency in Minneapolis. I had never dreamed of living in Minnesota, but I jumped at the opportunity.

In December 1992, I drove the very used Honda Civic hatchback I'd purchased with a $5,000 "start your life" loan from my mom and drove 1,700 miles over 25 hours. This was before Google Maps, cell phones, or the internet. I drove the final eight hours in a snowstorm, slowly passing much bigger cars littering ditches and emergency lanes. I was terrified, but I persisted because I was determined to make it there by sunset on New Year's Day to be ready for my first day of work in my first professional job. I remember the moment I finally arrived and pulled into the driveway of the poorly furnished, tiny "house" that I had asked my new boss to help me find in the local newspaper's classified ads. I looked around and started to cry. What was I doing with my life?

Despite the shaky start, I loved living in Minneapolis and working at that agency, where I met friends and colleagues I would stay in touch with for decades. I developed a deeper understanding of professional services, which is what I've been doing for most of my career. It was the perfect starter job.

Within 18 months, however, a headhunter called to ask if I would be willing to live between Santiago, Chile, and Portland, Maine. Another marketing and public relations agency in Maine needed a Spanish-speaking account executive to tend to its client, the Foreign Affairs Ministry of Chile. Again, I jumped at the chance. I loved the idea of living overseas and using my Spanish language skills in my daily work. This time, in the same Honda Civic, my mom and I drove 1,500 miles to Maine, another state that hadn't been on my original bucket list.

I commuted for months at a time between continents, hosting American journalists and touring the country as they wrote about travel, trade, and investment in Chile. I felt inexperienced for an international job with this level of responsibility, and I worked around the clock trying to find my way as I engaged with corporate executives, government officials, and members of the media. I was always the youngest woman in the room, and usually the only woman not in an administrative role. Over many trips to Chile, however, I realized that being a young American woman was an advantage. I didn't fall prey to the same cultural stereotypes that Chilean women did, and many very senior Chileans gave me the benefit of the doubt, allowing me the access, support, and opportunity to prove myself.

Nearly 30 years later, I reflected on that experience again as Carla Harris and I talked about her own experience as the "only" on Wall Street as she rose in the ranks at Morgan Stanley:

If you're the only one who looks like you in the room . . . you're the *only* one who looks like you in the room! It's an asset, not a liability. You do not have to vie for attention. When you speak, everybody will look, and all you have to do is deliver your excellence right into the opportunity. It's an honor and a privilege to be the "only"; I will try to make your experience with me so fabulous that you will ascribe whatever that is to the next person you see who looks like me.

Along with Carla, Molly Fletcher is another one of the boldest women I know and a role model when it comes to taking risks without fear of failure. Today she's an acclaimed keynote speaker, author, and podcaster, but she built her brand as the female Jerry Maguire, one of the only women cutting her teeth in the 1990s in the highly competitive sports agent industry. She has told wildly compelling stories on our stages at the Women in Leadership Institute™ about her fearlessness.

For example, in her early twenties, she cold-called the famous Zig Ziglar, an author and founding father of the motivational speaking industry. She secured a meeting and then booked a plane ticket from Michigan to Dallas, where she entered his office to seek his counsel about how she could emulate his rise as a keynote speaker. His advice: "Molly, why don't you go do something first, and then maybe you can go talk about it." So, she followed her passion in the sports business. A few years later, she worked her way into a sports agency in Atlanta as a marketing coordinator and slowly found her niche, convincing the owner to shift his business development strategy to focus on specific sports. She quickly jumped into recruiting and signing baseball players, then navigated into college basketball coaches, and then golfers and broadcasters. She secured more than 300 clients and developed a full team of agents supporting the talent. In short, she built a business and a brand through pure grit and resilience. And now, she is the author of five books, a sought-after keynote speaker on leadership and peak performance, and an award-winning podcaster.

It's easy to admire the Carla Harrises and Molly Fletchers of the world from afar, but leaning into the fear and trying new things is how we build our confidence in the value we create. And when we believe in ourselves, others will believe in us, too. We can do that when we take on a stretch assignment, lead a project, switch jobs, start a business, write a book, or choose to stay home and raise our kids. What is the risk you are willing to take today?

Fail Fast and Try Again

Things don't always work out, and that's okay. Sometimes the best way to recognize your value and accomplishments is to learn from failure and try again.

When CEB, the publicly traded firm I was at for eight years, sold to Gartner in 2017, I knew the business unit I was leading was at risk of being spun off or shut down altogether. The truth is, I had been unhappy in my evolving role for much of the prior year, so I activated my external network and secured a job quickly at one of the world's largest leadership development companies. I couldn't believe my luck and timing. I figured I would stay at this firm for the remainder of my career. It all fell into place easily and seemed too perfect. And it was.

My sponsor, whom I'll call Ray, had been a mentor to me as an executive at my previous company and had opened the door for me at the new firm, but there were a lot of unknowns. The position had never existed before, and he was building the business unit from scratch, so there wasn't a job description or an established team structure, as roles were still being defined. Also, I learned Ray wouldn't be my direct manager, and I didn't particularly like the guy who would be my actual boss (to be fair, I don't think he liked me, either, because he didn't really have a say in my hiring). But I overlooked all those things because I had such respect and admiration for Ray. I trusted the unknowns would all work out over time as I helped grow the business and culture.

It was a disaster from the start. Within three weeks, Ray announced he was leaving the organization after only six months due to a reorganization at the top. As a result, I was lost. The role I was promised never manifested.

I had no direct reports, no authority, and no personal brand inside the company. The culture was soul-sucking to me, and it seemed everyone was out for themselves. I hung on for six months, unhappy, despondent, and desperately trying to find my way, until my husband gave me a wake-up call. He said, "The family needs our Mommy back." I was stuck and taking the failure so personally that I had lost focus on what was far more important to me. Using a lot of guidance from my advisors, I forced their hand and was laid off. It was over. A complete failure.

Except that it wasn't. That's when I took my self-proclaimed sabbatical (described in detail in chapter five), during which time, a headhunter from the very same leadership organization I had left found me and asked if I would consider the CEO role at Linkage. Had I not failed at that job, the door for this one—the very best job I have ever had—would have stayed closed forever.

Failure doesn't feel good, especially in the moment, but moving forward and not taking it personally is a skill that can be beneficial. My colleague Kristen Howe and I have worked together for more than a decade. When I ran the Leadership Academies business at CEB, she was one of our top facilitators and traveled the world delivering leadership training to HR, IT, and finance leaders from large organizations. I remember how nervous she was to deliver in Europe, as the participants were notoriously more critical and always scored our programs lower than did those who took our programs in North America or Asia. To make matters worse, she was the only female facilitator with a group of all-male finance leaders in London.

Her fear was well founded, and she received difficult feedback around the content and the delivery on top of negative comments about why our company exported American facilitators all the way to Europe to teach leadership. Kristen called me at the end of her first day completely distraught. Understandably, she did not want to deliver the second half of the session the following day. But she regrouped in her hotel room, created a plan that took some of the feedback into account, and held her head high as she marched back into the classroom. Experiences like that helped her master her craft and become one of the best facilitators I have ever seen.

Develop a Support System

Remember, recognized confidence is about how you put yourself out there in the world so that *others* see the value you bring. When it's hard to see your own value, sometimes you need to phone a friend. That could mean taking a risk to be vulnerable and ask for help. Unlike "faking it 'til you make it," this shows your human side, and you will certainly be rewarded because people who care about you most often see your value much more clearly than you do.

Chester Elton is a treasured fellow member of my Marshall Goldsmith 100 Coaches network. He is known in our group as the "Apostle of Appreciation," not only because he and his longtime business partner, Adrian Gostick, authored the bestseller *Leading with Gratitude* but also because he lives and loves with gratitude—it's a core principle that guides his life. As a result, everyone loves Chester. He is one of the kindest, most generous, and most accomplished leaders I know, and I've been privileged to collaborate with him over the last several years. So, it came as a bit of a surprise on a summer day in 2022 when I, along with 18 other people in Chester's close circle, received this text:

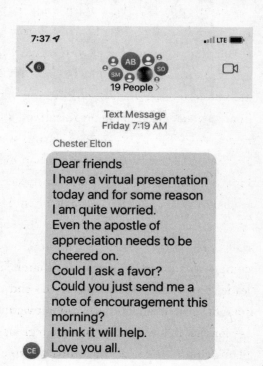

I was up early that morning, so I saw it when it came in at 7:19 AM and responded immediately (below left).

What was most fascinating, and inspiring, was watching all the responses funnel in immediately after mine (below right).

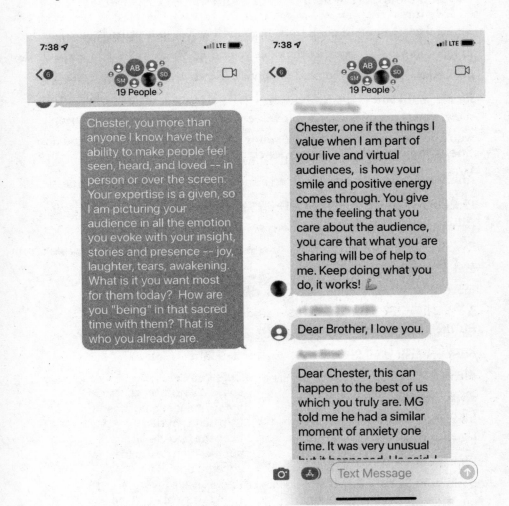

The texts went on and on throughout the day—memes, quotes, words of encouragement—but mostly acknowledgment of Chester's Superpowers and his impact. That is what recognized confidence is. And Chester's actions reinforced it.

My initial reaction was shock that the famous Chester Elton needed help at all, but his act of courage gave me greater pause. He *asked* for it so publicly and *received* it so lovingly. Had I ever done that? Had I ever seen any woman do that? Chester had provided an exceptional teaching moment for me, and I vowed to use his strategy the next time I felt like an imposter.

Speak the Language of Confidence and Project Your Individual Wins

Once you've tried new things, failed a few times, and built up a strong support system that reminds you of your value even when you can't quite see it yourself, it's time to stop apologizing and downplaying your excellence and begin promoting your wins! For others to recognize our confidence, we must demonstrate that we know our value.

Even on the tennis court, I see women use self-deprecating, apologetic language that portrays uncertainty or minimizes accomplishments. When our opponent double-faults, my partner will often apologize: "It was out, sorry." When I praise a player for a well-placed winner, she will almost always downplay her achievement with, "I just got lucky." At the office, it's even more common. Most of the time when I publicly acknowledge a woman on my team for an excellent outcome or idea, the deferential response is, "It was all about the team." All this couching and padding and positioning is exhausting, and it's not effective, either.

That said, this posture is part of our upbringing, our values, and our identity, so it's hard to change—and it's not a bad thing to be humble and highlight our teams. But women in large part do not need to work on lifting and promoting others; we're already good at it, and we should continue to do so. This is about balance. Think about the last 30 days. How many times during that period have you publicly lifted other people or teams versus yourself?

There are ways to take appropriate credit for what you have accomplished and share it with others. In fact, it's a critical part of managing your brand.

Find Appropriate Ways to Demonstrate Your Own Contribution

A few times a year at most companies, we can highlight our accomplishments through the often-dreaded performance review process. While it's a good forum for documenting success, women need to make their contributions visible much more frequently, highlighting their role in wins that are aligned with the personal brand they want to convey. If you want to be seen as strategic, then find ways to lead a strategy session or articulate the strategic evolution of a project you manage. If you get exceptional feedback from a client, send it to your boss with a note about how the feedback aligns with the outcomes of the important projects you've been working on.

I've noticed that women tend to share with me the exceptional work of others on their teams and give credit to the collective but share less often about themselves. Our corporate intranet site, called the Watercooler, is full of examples of women highlighting others' efforts and outcomes. I love it, and it supports our strong team culture. However, especially with their managers, women need to take the credit and communicate the value they bring. We've already discussed that most women are uncomfortable talking about themselves, so here are a few ideas to make this whole thing easier.

One simple solution is to have others talk about your accomplishments, even if you have to ask them to do so. This is especially effective if people in positions of power and influence are singing your praises. This is where a bit of vulnerability comes in, the kind Chester showed us. It might look like approaching a trusted colleague or even your manager to say, "I'm proud of the customer feedback I just received, and I'd like to make it visible to the next level of leadership, but I'm concerned about it being perceived as arrogant. Could I ask you to help me?"

A second approach is to create and distribute unique content.

Dorie Clark is another member of our 100 Coaches network and a world-class author, speaker, and recognized Top 50 business thinker in the world. She is a master at self-promotion, and I have long admired her work and impact as an expert in "self-reinvention" and helping others make changes in their lives. In a 2018 *Harvard Business Review* article, she offered an idea about how to promote yourself and demonstrate your expertise:

> Many women may feel uncomfortable talking about their accomplishments and promoting themselves directly. But there are other ways to show your areas of expertise when building a brand. Content creation is a good way to share your ideas and build a positive reputation at scale. The precise mechanics will differ based on company policies (your ability to use social media may be limited in certain regulated industries, for instance), but in almost any organization, there are ways that [you can demonstrate] your knowledge and help others.[7]

Dorie herself whips out blogs, podcasts, articles, and books faster than anyone I know. And if you haven't joined her newsletter distribution list, head to dorieclark.com now.

The final way is the easiest and most effective, and that is to find natural ways to weave your achievements into conversations, emails, and meetings. There is a good balance to strike in terms of the medium, frequency, and approach of doing so.

Here's a perfect example from Kristen, who sends me a casual email every week or so to offer up specific news about her progress and impact. She's been doing this for decades:

> At my former company, I'd send an email to my boss, Nathan, at least once a week with a few accomplishments that I knew he

wasn't aware of. This was during a $4 billion post-merger integration, and we were the acquired company, so it wasn't easy for him to know everything. I also found ways to be valuable to him. I knew so many people across our legacy organization, and I was building new relationships as I navigated the new one. I'd often email Nathan with the line "I have some information for you." One day he showed up after one of my emails and said, "You are better than the CIA—you know everything!" Instead of downplaying or deferring, I said, "I cultivate relationships wherever I go, and people tell me things because of it. I'm trustworthy and knowledgeable, so people want to be in my orbit."

I also love the example of Melissa Turk, a product manager on our Linkage team, who joined us just a few months before our all-company offsite in 2022. Due to the COVID-19 pandemic, we hadn't been together in person for 28 months, so we wanted to integrate some ice breakers and team-building exercises throughout the agenda. Melissa volunteered to help and told her boss, "I'd love to help—I'm very good at creating innovative team exercises and have led really well-received openers in the past." That was straightforward self-promotion. It got the executive team's attention and made us comfortable she could get the job done. More important, it secured recognized confidence in Melissa by the executive team. A few months later, at our semiannual talent calibration conversation, her role in the offsite surfaced as proof of Melissa's early contribution and capability.

We've established that self-promotion is a necessary part of everyone's job. For others to see your confidence on display, you need to master the art of telling others in power the value you've created. However, there are some downsides—no one likes someone who brags all the time, even if they are getting the work done. In conjunction with the tactics we've already discussed, let's get specific on how to promote ourselves gracefully.

⁂ ACT NOW
How to Build Your Recognized Confidence

When done well, self-promotion is very powerful. Here is a short quiz to help you understand your current level of self-promotion. Use this scoring system:

1= never; 2 = sometimes; 3 = regularly

How Often Do You:

* Tell someone more senior than you about an accomplishment of yours?
* Consider self-promotion part of your job?
* Regularly schedule an informal chat with someone senior to you to discuss your future?
* Send your boss an email detailing one accomplishment of yours from the week?
* Ask to lead an initiative with the rationale that "I am very good at this"?
* Tie your self-promotion to the value to the organization?

Scoring: 18 is the top score. Consider how you scored and reflect on where you can improve it.

How to Construct a Self-Promotion Snapshot

Self-promotion can take many forms: a quick email to your boss, a long conversation about your strengths with someone in power, or a 60-second elevator ride with the CEO. You need to be ready for whenever the opportunity comes your way.

A good approach is to construct your comments in multiple layers, like the cake on the next page. The foundation is the accomplishment itself, followed by three things: the specific role you played, the impact on the organization, and why it is important to you.

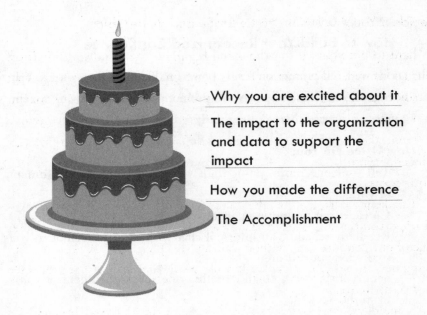

Why you are excited about it

The impact to the organization
and data to support the
impact

How you made the difference

The Accomplishment

At a former job, Kristen found herself sharing the elevator with the CEO upon returning to the office after a two-day trip to Paris visiting an important client. He asked how her week was going.

That open-ended question can be difficult to answer, but she leaned into it as an opportunity to self-promote. Instead of saying "I had a great trip to Paris visiting a client," she took a deep breath and said, "I just came back from Paris, where I upsold a client engagement from a two-day program to a six-day program. I shared how the experience was applicable to their team and created a much broader program for them and more revenue for us. The current account manager hadn't been able to move them to the larger program without someone with deeper product expertise, so I was so glad that I could. I'm excited to use my experience to influence our clients." Even in seemingly small, inconsequential encounters, there are opportunities to share your value.

Decide If You Are Willing to Be Brave and Vulnerable

It's hard to put yourself out there and highlight the value and impact of your accomplishments. But worse than the challenge of doing so is what we risk by avoiding these opportunities. This quote from Dr. Gotian can serve as a warning sign: "If you let the feeling of being labeled as a phony or fraud take control, you will subconsciously alter your goals to protect yourself, minimizing your accomplishments and potentially sabotaging future success."

I make it a personal goal for myself and my staff to find developmental opportunities and stretch experiences that will keep us on the outer edge of our comfort zone without falling over the edge. Taking risks and trying new things is a way to build your confidence and ensure others see your competence.

Some days, your best won't be good enough, and your Inner Critic will berate you: *I'm not qualified. I'm not on track. I'm not worthy.* In those moments, reach out to others who care about your success and get a boost from them. Ask for support to reignite your spark, and ensure that others see your efforts, too. It is the daily pursuit of your potential that generates the personal satisfaction of knowing you are giving it your all. In those moments when I'm questioning whether the work I'm doing is "enough," or whether I'm "enough," I remember what I learned from Harry Kraemer, former CEO of Baxter and professor of management and strategy at Northwestern University's Kellogg School of Management. At the end of each day, he asks two questions as his guiding principles for a day well lived: "Did I do what I thought was right? Did I do my best?"

If the answer is yes to both, you are doing just fine.

8

Branding & Presence—Show Up the Way You Wish to Be Known

RATE YOURSELF (1–5)

In day-to-day work as a leader, I . . . Present and actively manage a professional image.					
Rarely Demonstrate 1	Sometimes Demonstrate 2	Often Demonstrate 3	Very Often Demonstrate 4	Almost Always Demonstrate 5	N/A
○	○	○	○	○	○

I can't think of one woman in my life who isn't striving to be great at her job. But as we discussed in the previous chapter, just doing our jobs well isn't enough for us to advance as leaders. We need to build our credibility in the areas we want to be known for by not only establishing our competence through doing our work consistently well but also by gaining other people's recognition and approval for doing so. That means "showing up" in the way that you want to be seen—in your full authenticity—and getting very curious about what people share about you behind closed doors.

Please reflect for a moment: How often do you pause long enough to consider your personal leadership brand and whether you are operating authentically? Do you seek or receive feedback on how others perceive you? And do you intentionally create opportunities to reinforce the brand you wish to be known for?

It's not surprising if your answer to all these questions is a reluctant no. We're more practiced at obscuring or at least downplaying our true selves than purposely projecting them! We discussed the importance of self-promotion in the last chapter on Recognized Confidence, which is about our accomplishments. Branding & Presence is a close sister, focused on our authentic selves and our leadership brand.

Starting in middle school, women tend to spend a lot of time worrying about what others think of them. We may stop raising our hands because we don't want to get the answer wrong or appear too smart. We take great care to model our appearance after the cool girls at school or in the media. We may even start to conceal parts of ourselves that might make others uncomfortable, like our sexuality, religion, ethnicity, or disability. By the time we enter the workforce, most women have learned how to assimilate into male-dominated norms, impacting everything from the way we dress and wear our hair to what we choose to share about our lives outside the workplace (often including motherhood), all in an effort to "fit in." This is especially true for women of color who struggle with the triple bind of layering race and ethnicity on top of the challenges of being a woman leader in a world where even fewer people at the top look like them.

I mentioned in chapter four on Internal Bias that we recently interviewed Marilu Galvez, president and general manager of WABC-TV in New York. During that conversation, she relayed to more than 800 webinar registrants how she had "covered" her Latina heritage for decades by straightening her hair, tapering her vivacious personality, and withholding information about her upbringing in a multigenerational home of strong women. She evolved into leading authentically as she moved into greater positions of authority, and she became more comfortable embracing her identity as a Latina.

She offhandedly noted to the virtual audience that she eventually allowed her hair to go "free" in all the glory of her natural curls, even recounting how devastated she was when a colleague commented, "Marilu forgot to brush her hair this morning." I was a little surprised when the Zoom chat erupted immediately with women offering similar examples and encouragement to each other about their hair—going gray, curly, braided—but I knew there was a deeper meaning. We want to be our authentic selves in every aspect of our lives, including at work. We no longer accept hiding who we really are.

WHAT IS BRANDING & PRESENCE, EXACTLY?

Essentially, your *brand* is the reputation you create for yourself as a leader, how people picture you. *Presence* is how your reputation manifests when you engage with others. Brand and presence are inextricably linked as the total experience that others have of you across your collective interactions, either in person or virtually, in large groups or one-on-one. Over time, this experience creates others' perceptions of both your competence—your capabilities and expertise—and your leadership presence, or how you "show up." It's how people see you, and, ideally, their perception of you should be aligned with who you really are at your core.

While all the hurdles weave together, the focus on Branding & Presence presupposes that you have already done some work on overcoming the others. The order of the hurdles, in this book and in our development programs, is linear. To effectively manage your leadership brand, it's important to have first addressed a few others:

- ✳ **Clarity:** You want people to recognize you in conjunction with your aspiration, which is what you are moving toward.
- ✳ **Proving Your Value:** Instead of being known for saying yes to everything, the work you lead should be aligned to what you want to be known for.
- ✳ **Recognized Confidence:** This requires promoting your accomplishments so people see your strengths and potential in those areas that feed your brand.

Even if we're clear on what we want to be known for, ensuring people see us as we want to be seen isn't easy, especially in a digital-first environment. Our world is noisy, we're all distracted, and it takes a lot of intention to ensure that we're embracing our own competence and authenticity—and projecting that to others. If we're actively working to craft and promote our brand, there is a much greater likelihood that our competence will be recognized by others. And when we project our brand authentically, it helps people know us and trust us, which is critical to landing a new assignment, job, or customer.

There are many ways to convey our brand and presence, and they all merit our awareness and attention:

- ✳ **The things we say and do, which reveal our character:** Do you tell the truth, meet deadlines, and keep promises? Are you driven and hardworking? Helpful and empathetic?
- ✳ **The things we write:** How do you offer your perspectives, opinions, and expertise through email, notes, blogs, articles, or books?
- ✳ **Our social media presence:** How do you find and influence the people you most want to engage—on LinkedIn, Twitter, Instagram, Facebook, or TikTok?
- ✳ **The people and groups we affiliate with:** Are you in networking circles, affinity groups, communities of interest, or volunteer projects that support the brand you want to convey?

✳ **How we express ourselves through our office, clothing, and appearance:** Are these things authentic to you, and do you feel your uniqueness is honored and accepted within the broader organizational brand?

Because our brand and presence are reflected in how others perceive us, it is important to ask for—and graciously accept—feedback regularly, especially from people who see you in action professionally. As my friend and mentor Marshall Goldsmith has taught me and millions of others through his own writing, coaching, and speaking, the only appropriate response to any feedback is, "Thank you."

WHY IS BRANDING & PRESENCE A HURDLE FOR WOMEN?

Here's one of the biggest challenges women leaders have faced throughout history: When women move into leadership roles, we look around at the leadership majority across nearly every industry and do not see others who look, or lead, like us. We often don't fit naturally into the expected mold. So, we are forced to make a choice: either contort ourselves to make *others* more comfortable or embrace our own leadership style and make *ourselves* more comfortable—but risk not being accepted. This decision is where your brand and your authenticity meet.

Just a decade ago, it was much harder for women to be authentic in leadership roles. Many of us have been balancing who we are with who we're expected to be throughout our careers, and there have been real consequences for our choices. If we didn't contort ourselves, maybe we didn't get the job, promotion, raise, or recognition because we weren't seen as having "leadership potential" or because we were too "different."

We are now at a unique turning point. When the world stopped in 2020, we were suddenly thrown together alongside our colleagues in a virtual environment, all trying to figure out how to navigate a new way of working and a new way of being. Like Marilu, we had more freedom and flexibility to experiment with our own leadership brand while embodying our authentic selves in the hybrid workplace. There was no time or energy, or even a physical office environment, to pretend or contort any longer, and that created some freedom and flexibility. It also helped others see us demonstrating our natural strengths and uniqueness, on the screens at work and in social media. We are now entering an era when organizations and leaders, who may not look like us, are beginning to understand the value of our difference.

We need to consider our brand and know that we can operate most effectively at work when we can embrace our true selves. When you become clear about where you want to go professionally and how you want people to see you, look for the places where you can add value as well as the places that value you for who you are.

WHAT HAS CHANGED IN THE LAST FEW YEARS?

In Linkage's data set that we've tracked for many years, the Branding & Presence hurdle is the one that women struggle with the least. This suggests that women have largely cleared the hurdle. Good news, right?

But questions remain: Is the image we're projecting *truly* one that reflects our authentic selves? Or are we continuing to hide any parts that may not be acceptable (or at least comfortable) to the leadership majority? The time is right for us to make more headway in striving to be true to ourselves in every area of life—and it would be a shame to miss our moment.

The rules that have governed leadership historically are changing, and women are well positioned in this new environment. Across the years of the COVID-19 pandemic, the "command and control" leadership style simply did not work, given the ambiguity and complexity of the intense challenges that paralyzed businesses and their employees. It took courage for leaders to admit they didn't have all the answers, and collaboration to engage everyone in solving problems we had never seen before.

The leaders who emerged as most successful were those who operated with an evolving set of capabilities that women have become adept at very naturally over generations—inclusion, vulnerability, empathy, trust, and transparency, to name a few. This shift is welcome news, and it gives us more "permission" to show up authentically and increases the likelihood that we will be understood, accepted, and rewarded for it.

However, being seen and known in your authenticity still requires visibility. It's unlikely that others are going to simply thrust us into the spotlight! Women need to lean into the discomfort of ensuring that others are aware of our natural leadership strengths. For those of us working in a hybrid environment, it is easier to hide and harder to stand out. When working from home, we need to consider how we show up with different audiences, and that includes how we engage on our screens—our computer background, our decision to be present on video, our ability to participate actively, and even our appearance. It may be okay at times to be an observer on an internal group call with your peers, but how are you heard or seen when you are in a virtual space with your leaders? How prepared are you for the call? What value do you add? What is the image you want to convey? Is it appropriate for your role and in alignment with the company image?

The intertwined nature of brand and presence is unavoidable. When you choose to step into the light as a high-potential, high-performing leader, how you "show up" is judged in every interaction. It is up to you to ensure you are demonstrating the skills that not only bring value to the organization but also match how you want to be most valued. When your intention and impact align, people perceive your Superpowers, and you become known for them.

BRANDING & PRESENCE IN REAL LIFE

In the evolving complexity of our world, when answers are not black and white and the expectations of leadership are changing, we can release the burden of leading in a way we have seen others do in the past. It's time to stop hiding who we really are, unleash our authentic selves, and embrace our uniqueness and natural strengths. Just as we've discussed the importance of ensuring that others recognize our accomplishments, we need to manage our own leadership brand to ensure the way others see us aligns to what we most want them to see. Here's how we can do it.

Identify Your Brand and Share Your Intention

At our virtual company kickoff in early 2022, my colleague Shannon Bayer led an important session on everyone's individual role in creating and sustaining the kind of culture we need to thrive at our organization. As part of the session, we gave the staff an opportunity to think about their individual brand and discuss in small groups of three how they wanted to be perceived at work. Then, their colleagues offered ideas about how to strengthen each person's brand, especially if their intention wasn't aligned to how others saw them. It was a simple but effective self-reflection exercise with an opportunity for peer feedback.

I was grouped with two team members I don't have the opportunity to interact with daily, and it was an honor to hear them articulate their desired brands:

Jim, a 24-year veteran of our organization in the finance function, wanted to be known as the company historian, the keeper of knowledge, and a calm sounding board.

Serena, a member of our customer success team, wanted to be seen as a thoughtful and reliable expert who managed every detail of customer engagement.

The words I came up with for my role as CEO were inspiring, engaging, and authentic. I went a step further and crafted a statement about how I hoped my staff talked about me when I wasn't in the room. I shared it with them to get a sense of how it felt to say it out loud:

She is an inspiring, engaging, authentic CEO. She is clear about our aspiration and strategic about our focus to ensure Linkage thrives. She is committed to achieving our goals, and she makes me feel like an important contributor to our success.

It didn't take me long to craft those words because it was the articulation of how I had been trying to lead. It felt important to set that intention and share it with others. Different from clarity, which is the vision for the "what" you want to create, your brand is *how* you want to be perceived while you're working to achieve your aspiration. It can provide a clear focus and help you recalibrate in moments when you feel unsure of yourself or when your Inner Critic is in One Down.

Am I Being the Leader I Want to Be Right Now?

If we're not careful, our brand can devolve into a reflection of how others see us when we aren't operating at our best. And it's not always clear what "our best" is. For example, across my entire life, a part of my identity has been the "hardworking achiever." It was something that I valued and was rewarded for in my family, in school, and in my early career as an individual contributor. It probably helped when I was a driven student, striving for stellar grades and working multiple jobs to buy special things my parents couldn't afford or to pay my portion of college tuition. It likely also helped me as I tried to gain experience and build my résumé, determined to prove myself and get promoted or to change jobs and increase responsibility.

Interestingly, in the early years of my career, it never occurred to me to reflect on how I was showing up. I also didn't stop to consider using my work experiences to determine where my strengths and passion aligned. I just wanted to succeed, at any cost. However, as early as my mid-twenties, when I became a leader of teams and projects, I started to see how my hard-driving ambition was preventing me from being the type of leader and person I ultimately aspired to be.

Back at the Coca-Cola Company, I was responsible for leading our public relations efforts for the 1998 Olympic Winter Games in Nagano, Japan. As in many of my early roles, I was in over my head without a lot of guidance. On this project, I was directly responsible for dozens of radio deejays that Coca-Cola had invited to broadcast from the Games as well as a large technology crew supporting our efforts and other employees under my direction.

We had all received tickets to the Opening Ceremonies, but after the event, despite the late hour and the frigid temperatures, Coca-Cola's hospitality director Klaus asked us to get off the transportation Coca-Cola had provided to make room for our customers. In retrospect, it was a very reasonable request, but I protested. Still, Klaus demanded that we find other transport home. Instead of pausing and trying to collaborate with him, I dug in my heels and refused to ask my tired crew to get off the bus. The radio deejays cheered me on, grateful for the ride, but deep down I knew I had made a mistake. While Klaus was a peer, he had a lot of influence with senior executives.

Mary, a beloved and respected colleague who had been in my role previously, pulled me aside later and asked me a few important coaching questions that I still remember: "How do you want to be viewed as a leader? Was it worth it to risk your reputation with Klaus, knowing you need his support not only for these Olympic Games but for every subsequent event you lead while here at Coca-Cola? What can you do now to repair the relationship?"

I was embarrassed, and I apologized to Klaus for my behavior. There was nothing wrong with being hard-driving and negotiating for my team, but I had done so at the expense of an important relationship. What's more, I was inadvertently developing a brand that could hurt me over time: if I became known as unyielding or uncooperative, nobody would want to work with me. This feedback was critical, and it has stuck with me my entire life. It helped me realize that preserving and deepening relationships at work needed to be a priority for me, more so than short-term wins. Had Mary not taken the time to gently point out the potential consequences of my behavior, I don't think I would have recognized that my behavior was significantly out of alignment with how I wanted to be perceived. When she called attention to it, I acted swiftly.

Take the Feedback and Use It to Evolve Your Brand

Feedback may be a gift, but it's often hard to embrace and act upon. Our brains are wired to shut down when receiving negative feedback. But if you can stay open to it, and even thank those offering it, feedback can support you in evolving your leadership brand.

After many years of success running the Leadership Academies at CEB, I had a difficult performance review in 2014. I was still running the business unit I had taken over in 2010, but growth was slowing, and we were dependent on our global sales team for success. I had no authority over the sales leaders but I had to influence them, which was hard because our incentives were different. I was held to profitability metrics, while they were goaled on top-line bookings, so I had to ensure that the scope and pricing of the solutions met our margin targets. Conversely, they wanted to sell at any cost. We were often at odds, and I would usually stand my ground to protect my team, especially when times were tough.

It's never good management practice to surprise your employees during a review, but I was completely shocked to learn from my manager that these executives, who were all men and outranked me, saw me as "difficult to work with" and "uncollaborative." Collaboration is a core value for how I operate in the world, and I had to really dig deep to determine why I was showing up differently. Was it the misaligned incentives that prevented either team from getting what we wanted and needed from the business negotiations? Was it a classic case of the double bind, where as a woman leader I was perceived as too aggressive? Or was it really me—something I needed to work on, given my competitive nature and perennial drive to succeed?

I was humiliated when my boss and the head of HR assigned me an executive coach to help overcome the issues that were preventing me from further success in my role. They positioned it as an honor, but it felt like a punishment. Nonetheless, I thanked them for the development opportunity and offered gratitude for the investment the company was making in me as a leader.

Working with the coach, I focused on slowing down and listening more openly to others outside of my own business unit. I tried to be less protective of my own team and goals and look at the bigger picture of what was best for the organization. As I did this, I articulated my intention verbally. When I met with the very same people who had given me the tough feedback, I would say things like, "I'd like to collaborate with you to resolve this issue to find what's best for both teams" or, "Collaboration is important to me, so I'd like to hear what you think is the best way forward." My hope was that, over time, their perception of me would change.

Asking others—especially those who are objective or care about your success—how they would describe your leadership is a good way to determine if you are evolving into the leader you want to be. Or, like I did, you can wait for the critical feedback that will jump-start your evolution. Either way, you'll get the opportunity. What's most important is that you remain open to the feedback, however it comes about.

Manage Your Brand Proactively

In spring 2022, I was contacted by a recruiter for an interesting role—to lead the North American business unit of a well-known Europe-based leadership development firm that was investing in digital innovation. My philosophy is to take select calls like this when they come around because they are exceptional opportunities to understand what is out there in the job market, learn more about the industry and our competitors, and determine what the hiring organization sees as the unique value I can bring. In short, because someone in your network has inevitably recommended you to the recruiter, these types of calls are perfect chances to perform a check-in on your brand.

After reading the job profile and doing some quick research on the company, I jumped on an introductory call to learn more about the company's evolution and the open executive position. Simon, the British recruiter, was friendly and casual, so I felt comfortable asking him why he thought I would be right for the role they had struggled to fill. I was shocked at the amount of preparation he had done but was equally surprised with his response. He said, "I did some research and talked to several people who know you. The words that came up were 'measured,' 'considered,' 'passionate,' and 'strategic.'"

I paused, wondering about the British interpretation of the words "measured" and "considered." To me, those words mean "slow" or "analytic"—neither of which resonated with me or would be words I'd choose to describe myself. So, I asked him to clarify, and while he gave me additional detail, the description still didn't fully resonate. Instead of protesting, I thanked him for his efforts and chose to see the conversation as a gift because it prompted me to manage my own brand; it was mine to own.

After some reflection time, I followed up with him in an email:

> Thank you for the work you did in advance to prepare for our conversation and ask others about my leadership style. I liked the adjectives you presented; it is the combination of inspiring and engaging, along with organized process and execution, that I believe best captures my Superpowers. I hadn't ever heard the words "considered" or "measured" when describing me . . . but in this context, I can see how that rings true.

The specific words I chose were important—if I want people to see me as inspiring and engaging, I need to declare that as part of my brand efforts and demonstrate it in my words and actions.

Don't Let Your Digital Brand Be Defined for You

In this digital environment, the footprints we leave will define us, regardless of whether we choose to brand ourselves explicitly. I go straight to LinkedIn when I'm about to meet any new professional contact to get a sense of their background, role, and latest activity. That forms a quick impression about the person—how active are they in posting or commenting, and how does their profile represent their voice, expertise, and interests? I will then often do a Google search to see what else emerges that isn't carefully curated by them. I'm sure many others do the same.

My point is this: What you put out there digitally—and what others put out there about you, with or without your knowledge—is important. Ensure you are proactive about communicating regularly on at least one digital channel. It should be the channel where you are most likely to capture the attention of the people you want to reach professionally. For me, that is LinkedIn, but I'm aware that to continue my own brand evolution, I may need to develop a stronger presence on other platforms as well.

Social media is an excellent vehicle for demonstrating both your competence and your authenticity. I have found that the more personal and vulnerable I am in my public social media postings, the more people engage with my posts. People want to connect with you; they want to understand your character and your drive, and they want to see evidence of your personality, humor, and warmth. Increasingly, video is an excellent way to showcase all these traits, with short snippets shot on your cell phone and posted to social media.

If you're not sure how to get started with your social media presence, find a professional you admire, someone whose brand you might want to learn from, and let what they're doing inspire you to take the next step in promoting your own online presence. What is their unique voice? What do you like about their messages and tone? How often do they post and where? What ideas might you borrow and apply to your own evolving brand? There is nothing wrong with subtly emulating an approach that resonates with you as you build your own.

✳ **ACT NOW**
How to Build Your Brand & Presence

(Re)Discover Your Brand

If you haven't thought much about how you'd like to be perceived (your brand) compared to how you actually are perceived (your presence), here is an easy and actionable way to begin:

1. Write out five words that describe what you want your brand to be. If you are unsure, here are a few questions to guide your thinking:
   * How do people benefit from working with me?
   * What advice or help do people come to me for?
   * What do I do that makes me stand out from everyone else?
   * What makes the way I achieve results unique or interesting?
2. Text three people you work with who know you well and ask them for a few words that describe who you are at work. You may even ask them for how they believe you have added value to their lives, either personally or professionally. This will help deepen your understanding of how people see you.
3. Compare the lists. Consider:
   * Is my perception of my brand accurate?
   * Do others see me the way I want to be seen?
   * What could be causing a disconnect (if there is one)?
   * What evolution should I consider for my brand?

Evolve Your Brand & Presence

Once you discover how others currently perceive you, determine how it may need to evolve to align with where you want it to be. This will require action, and my colleague Kristen Howe did this at a critical point in her career. Here is her story:

When I was a newly promoted senior director at a large consulting firm, I realized I had to evolve both my brand and presence. Our company was very casual, but now I was being pulled into potential acquisition conversations with CEOs of other companies. Initially, I was intimidated in these meetings and didn't show up as someone with marketplace knowledge and insight. I knew that if I wanted to keep attending the meetings, I had to contribute meaningfully and make a mark.

I focused on my presence by preparing more, studying the external environment, and understanding the value drivers for my company. I prepared a few remarks, practiced them, then delivered them in the meeting with confidence. I also changed the way I dressed—from jeans and shirts to more business formal wear of slacks and blazers. While I don't want to focus on appearance, dressing differently helped me show up differently.

I hoped the work I was doing would extend to my brand and that I would become someone known for market intelligence, which would secure more invitations to meetings on acquisition targets. It worked. I was often called into meetings by the head of M&A instead of my boss because I had cultivated my brand to be of value in an area I had great interest in.

Find Ways to Articulate and Demonstrate Your Brand to Others

To articulate your brand to others, find appropriate ways to share the key adjectives you decided on and why they are important to you and the organization.

My brand is _____. The unique value I provide is important to the organization because _____.

Here are our examples:

Jennifer:

My brand is an inspiring, engaging, and authentic CEO in the women's leadership space. The unique value I provide is building and managing businesses that elevate women leaders and support organizations in becoming more inclusive.

Kristen:

My brand is an authentic, positive, calm executive leader who generates ideas to creatively solve problems. The unique value I provide is important to the organization because the strong followership and engagement I've created leads to better business outcomes.

Once you are clear about your brand, it's up to you to ensure people know it through your words and consistent actions. You can convey this when talking to others. I've heard Kristen offer in our team meetings, "If you need ideas on that topic, I'm happy to help. I am a good idea generator and creative problem solver."

For me, I engage the staff weekly at our business plan review meeting and always reground the group openly and honestly in our aspiration, asking how we are doing against our ambitious goals and whether our strategy is working. I publicly acknowledge the contributions individuals and teams have made. I am more aware now of when I am operating "off brand" and showing up in a way that is not authentic or aligned with my intentions. Now, instead of berating myself, I try and pause, tap into my Inner Coach, and overcome my Inner Critic to return to Compassionate Center.

Put Yourself Out There and Make Sure People Notice

We have to work consistently to ensure others see us in the way we intend. In Marshall Goldsmith's latest book, *The Earned Life*, he introduces the burden of building credibility twice. First, we need to establish our competence as something that other people value—and do it well on a consistent basis. Delivering on that promise creates trust.

But the second step is critical, and even harder for women. We need to gain recognition and approval for that competence *in order to* become influential and achieve our aspirations. These two modes of building credibility are independent variables—earning competence does not automatically guarantee that you will be recognized for that competence, which is why establishing and promoting our brand is so critical in this cluttered world where it's hard to be noticed.

Marshall has integrated four questions into his coaching to help us all overcome our fear of promoting our own brands. Watching him do this consistently over many years has inspired me to take more risk in putting myself out there publicly and authentically:

1. If I became more widely known as an expert in *women's leadership* [insert your own expertise here], could I make more of a positive difference in the world?
2. Does striving for this recognition make me uncomfortable?
3. Does my discomfort inhibit me and therefore limit my ability to make a positive difference?
4. Which is more important to me: my momentary discomfort or making a positive difference?

Marshall is one of the most well-known and well-branded leadership experts in the world, a reputation backed by the nearly 50 books he has authored or contributed to and the thousands of CEOs he has coached over four decades. When he talks about how he overcame his own reticence for self-marketing his brand, I listen. Let me close this chapter by offering Marshall's wise words here: "When I can convince myself that any uncomfortable task is for a greater good, my discomfort suddenly becomes a price I am happy to pay."

It requires considerable effort to build a brand, and it takes courage to receive feedback about how others perceive you. We continue to evolve with every breath, so this is work we'll undertake across our lifetimes. As your internal biases and clarity shift over time, so does your opportunity to align your focus and energy with how you most want to be seen and recognized. When you ultimately find yourself leading in a way that is completely "on purpose" and authentic to you—and others see you that way, too—it feels easier, and the results are better. That is a life well earned.

Making the Ask—Negotiate for What You Really Want

RATE YOURSELF (1–5)

In day-to-day work as a leader, I . . .					
Ask for what I want and need, with an expectation I may get it.					
Rarely Demonstrate 1	Sometimes Demonstrate 2	Often Demonstrate 3	Very Often Demonstrate 4	Almost Always Demonstrate 5	N/A
○	○	○	○	○	○

How often do you ask for something, big or small, for yourself? Not for your team or your family but for you? Women are not naturally conditioned to ask for what we want. We have for so long been working in supporting roles, helping men get what they want. Sometimes, in the workplace, it doesn't even occur to us that we *can* ask. When we do realize we want or need something, we may face a lot of fear and dread around asking for it, whether it's additional resources because a project load has become unbearable, flexibility during a particularly difficult time in our professional or personal lives, or even advice around an area where we need more expertise. I often hear women hesitating to ask for what they need, saying:

"I don't want to bother anyone."
"It will get better after this difficult time period."
"What I have now is good enough."
"I didn't know I could ask."

When I challenge women on what would happen if the situation were reversed, if their colleagues were to approach them with specific requests, they all agree they would hear them out and offer support willingly. In fact, many add they would be delighted, even honored, to be asked for help.

We women are so wired to please that we give freely to others but often don't stop to determine what *we* need, who can help us get it, and how to ask for those critical things that will get us closer to our deepest aspiration, the vision that emerges through clarity. It's time to change that.

WHAT IS MAKING THE ASK, EXACTLY?

Making the ask is all about pursuing what we really want and need. It's not about minimizing our needs and asking (or settling) for a lesser version of what we truly want, one we think will play well with the person on the receiving end of our request. And it's not only a strategy for critical conversations that occur at select and infrequent times, like when we negotiate a compensation package with a new job or approach a manager for a pay increase or title change.

We need to think much more broadly about what we are asking for and when. We should consistently and persistently ask for those things that would make the biggest difference in creating the career and life we most want: role evolution, stretch assignments, sponsorship or coaching, resources, work environment upgrades, flexibility, or even feedback and moral support.

When we integrate our asks into the natural course of our personal and professional life and practice frequently on both small and large asks, the entire process becomes less daunting and even fun.

WHY IS MAKING THE ASK A HURDLE FOR WOMEN?

Research has shown that women and men think of negotiating differently. Women perceive negotiating as something like a trip to the dentist—it's painful, we don't look forward to it, and perhaps we even dread it. While there is some gain afterward in the form of better, cleaner teeth, the trip itself is unappealing. Men, on the other hand, often think of negotiating as an exhilarating game. They're competing, playing to win, and enjoying the process itself.

In addition to the differing mindset, there are a few patterns I have found that women tend to struggle with uniquely:

* We aren't sure what we can ask for, so we either don't ask for anything at all or ask for a lesser version of what we want, thinking we're more likely to get it.
* We avoid conflict or confrontation in our efforts to please.
* We fear being told no and take it as a personal failure.
* We don't want to be seen as too ambitious or assertive and therefore less likable (remember the double bind that women face).
* If we are turned down at the first ask, we fear backlash or damage to the relationship, and so we don't continue the negotiation.

Much of this mindset stems from real external bias that we have internalized, which we discussed in chapter two. For example, according to the National Women's Law Center, the wage gap between men and women narrowed only by one penny in 2021, with full-time working women earning 84 cents for every dollar earned by men. For Black and Latina women, it is far worse, as they earn 67 and 57 cents, respectively, for every dollar earned by white, non-Hispanic men.[1] So what is going on here? Are women just poor negotiators? Are we just not ambitious or assertive enough? Or, when we do negotiate, do we actually face backlash because others perceive it as inappropriate for women to "behave aggressively"?

Research published in 2021 in the *Journal of Applied Psychology* (re-reported in *Forbes*) suggests it is the latter and that we are right to be concerned about the gender stereotypes that result in backlash against women who make strong requests.[2] The study, led by Dartmouth business professor Jennifer Dannals, examined more than 1,200 negotiation exercises and found that "gender differences in outcomes only emerged in one situation—when the female negotiator had a strong alternative." In those instances, according to the researchers, "a strong alternative might give women a justification for setting more ambitious targets, behaving more assertively, and claiming more value than they otherwise would." In that case alone, she was less likely to get the same outcome as a man because of the "unconscious bias that leads people to have certain expectations about how it's appropriate for men and women to behave." The conclusion: When women are more aggressive, they are less likely than men to get what they want.[3]

A 2022 *Harvard Business Review* article titled "Stop Undervaluing Exceptional Women" provides further evidence of external bias. Researchers found that highly qualified women are not only undervalued but are also taken for granted because of the assumption that women will be more loyal and less likely to job hop than highly qualified men, even if given a better career opportunity elsewhere. In addition, the article cites "mounting evidence that women hesitate to advocate for raises, more responsibility, or rewards for their work out of a concern that they'll be labeled bossy or arrogant when they do, and these concerns have merit. These labels have consequences because women face additional barriers to their career advancement when they're seen as unlikable, something that isn't true for men."[4]

The truth is we do face a double-edged sword: if we don't negotiate assertively, we may not achieve the same outcomes as those of our male counterparts; if we do, the backlash we may face can undermine our efforts anyway. That is disheartening because we can't control the unconscious bias of others, nor an organization's culture and values that allow this bias to permeate.

Still, the very real possibility of backlash is *not* reason enough to forego the ask. The more women who do this, the more normalized it will become. Also, living from a place of fear or dread in our current situation is not conducive to our career growth or our mental and emotional well-being in general. Even if our ask results in a no or there is fallout that results in the need for us to shift course, we will gain information that allows us to determine where to go from there.

WHAT HAS CHANGED IN THE LAST FEW YEARS?

The COVID-19 pandemic forced us to reevaluate what we want. We've either reemerged in new roles or made different decisions about where we work, how we work, and how much time we spend at work. And some women have even opted to leave the workforce altogether. Many industries are experiencing a critical talent shortage, and most companies acknowledge there is a specific dearth of women in the leadership ranks. With organizations publicly disclosing diversity metrics and struggling to fill open positions, women have more opportunity and power to ask for what we want—and we should expect to get it.

There is also a growing movement in boardrooms and executive suites to increase the number of women at the highest levels of leadership, with a special emphasis on women of color.[5] The diversity and equity arguments are finally being acknowledged and discussed more openly than ever before, and this spotlight gives women a unique window to embrace our own brand of leadership and negotiate for what we really want.[6]

MAKING THE ASK IN REAL LIFE

I have grown increasingly comfortable with making the ask as I've progressed in my career and developed more understanding about what I can ask for, along with gaining more experience and confidence in doing so.

As the CEO of Linkage until the sale of the company in late 2022, I reported to a private equity board. Even before starting the job, I made many asks while negotiating every detail of my employment contract—from salary, bonus, and equity to the number of weeks per month I would travel to our Boston headquarters from my Washington, DC, home. I hired a job coach to help me understand my market value and prioritize the areas where I could generate a more favorable outcome, as well as the areas I might want to let go. Having access to that experienced third party with an objective view allowed me to be bolder in my asks.

Once I got the job, I needed to make even more challenging asks: a capital raise for investment, staff bonus and retention plans, executive team compensation, reinstatement of full salaries after the 2020 downsizing, etc. I didn't get everything I wanted, but I've become a lot better about how and when I ask. I've learned how to gather data, build a business case where needed, find the right time and place, and understand where the other party is coming from. At Linkage, we have a whole course on how women can negotiate most effectively, which is critical given the double bind and the documented research on the backlash women may face if perceived as "too assertive" with their requests.

While asking does get easier with time and experience, here is one truth that's relevant at any age or career stage: If you don't ask, you are unlikely to get what you want. And if you really care about getting what you want, it is your responsibility to make the first move. A mistake that women often make is to keep our heads down and do exceptional work, believing someone will notice and spontaneously reward us (remember the Proving Your Value hurdle in chapter six and the Recognized Confidence hurdle in chapter seven?). In my experience, it doesn't work out that way. Most people, especially the men who hold 75 percent of executive positions,[7] are not aware, unprompted, of your needs and wishes, or of any real or perceived inequities in your situation. And it is human nature for most managers to pay attention to those who are actually making the ask, thereby making it impossible to ignore the actual requests brought to their attention.

Make Your Ask When the Opportunity Arises

In 2010, as the economy was still struggling to emerge out of the Great Recession, I was the senior director of product development for the Leadership Academies, an emerging business unit at CEB, which Gartner later acquired in 2017. The year before, after coming off maternity leave with my third child, I had chosen to pause my consulting firm, IntraVision, and return to the corporate world. The economy was spiraling, and after eight years of running my own business, I knew that I wanted to be back in a corporate environment, leading a team.

What I didn't know was that within a few months of my arrival, there would be significant layoffs at the firm, and those of us remaining would need to hunker down and rebuild our business unit, which had experienced a 90 percent decline in revenue across 2009. A very small group of exceptional professionals rallied together to save the business and serve the few clients that remained.

The climb was exhausting but exhilarating. My colleague Ed led the delivery team, and the two of us worked well together as the most senior leaders in a small business unit. About a year into our turnaround, however, Ed told me he planned to leave to become a contractor and focus on his passion, which was teaching leaders in the classroom versus running the day-to-day operations of the global delivery network. My boss, Nathan, began the effort to hire his replacement.

I loved having Ed as a colleague, but while I was disappointed to see him go, I quickly realized the potential that this change brought. I knew I had a short window of opportunity to move from owning a function—product development and management—to running the entire business unit as the general manager. It would be a big step up in responsibility, but I felt I was ready, and I knew my boss hadn't even considered it. I created a short business case, practiced my pitch, and marched into his office. It started with, "I'd like you to consider not replacing Ed because I believe I can run the business."

Nathan was surprised but open to the idea and agreed to try it. I spent the next four years in one of the best jobs I've ever had. Remember that executive MBA I thought I wanted while at Coca-Cola more than ten years before? Well, I got it on the job instead at CEB, learning to manage a P&L, create a shared vision, allocate resources, support and train a sales team, create operating efficiencies, and inspire a team of managers, who in turn built their own exceptional teams. I was compensated well and ultimately promoted to managing director.

To this day, I cite that simple ask as the key moment in gaining that first critical business management experience. When you see an opening that aligns to your clarity, grab it.

It's Never Too Early to Build Your Capability to Make the Ask

I was a 22-year-old graduate student in Stirling, Scotland, when I trudged out to the phone booth at 10 PM in the middle of a snowstorm, grasping a fistful of British coins. It was 5 PM in Atlanta, and my goal was to reach Frank Dean, the global head of sports marketing for Coca-Cola. I had done some pre-internet forensic work through college friends who had settled in Atlanta, and they had somehow surfaced his name and number. I saw Mr. Dean as my ticket to secure a job at the 1992 Olympic Games in Barcelona, which would help me with the access I needed to finish writing my master's thesis on how Olympic sponsors measured their return on sports sponsorship investments. I had one chance to make my case, and, miraculously, he picked up the phone himself on the first ring.

I remember the call vividly. I immediately started babbling enthusiastically about my program in Scotland, my Spanish language skills, my research, and my desire to support Coca-Cola at the Olympics and beyond. There was dead silence on the other end as I poured more coins into the payphone. And then he asked, "Who did you say you were?"

More than 30 years later, I still have the letter I sent him following our call. Please enjoy a verbatim excerpt:

Dear Mr. Dean:

I certainly enjoyed speaking to you last night, although we were in the midst of a snowstorm here in chilly Scotland and I was standing in a phone booth with the door almost frozen shut. I am more than willing, however, to make a few sacrifices if it will in any way help me to achieve my goals, and I felt like I got a step closer after our conversation. Thank you for giving me the advice and aid I needed as I attempt to secure a job with Coca-Cola this summer, and perhaps permanently in the near future.

The only barrier that remains is finding a way to get inside the organization during the Olympics in order to carry out my research. I have written Mr. Calvet, and I hope to speak to him when he returns to Madrid. However, often it is nearly impossible to get past the secretary in large companies in Spain, and I find it is easier working from the American end. That is why I was so relieved to get in touch with you, and I would greatly appreciate any further assistance you could give me.

I would be willing to work in any capacity during the summer months, and I would welcome any help or advice you could give me. I assume that my language skills would be an asset, as many American representatives from Coca-Cola will probably be arriving for the Games. My Rotary funding terminates in June, so it would be extremely helpful if I could get paid just enough for food

(and I don't eat much) for my work and research. However, if that
is not possible, I will work around that minor detail.

The full letter is two pages, single-spaced. I would certainly do it differently today, but in retrospect, I'm proud that I made three clear asks: (1) for
a summer position, (2) for the removal of the roadblocks I faced with the
Spanish leadership, and (3) for pay so I could eat. I got all three, and that
summer helped me build a network that charted the course of my profes-
sion for the next two decades.

Choose Your Timing and Your Medium of Communication Wisely

I realize that early in our careers, it's sometimes hard to know what we *can*
ask for, and knowing *how* to make the ask is equally mysterious.

As my daughter, Madeleine, began her college internship in 2022, she
wasn't convinced she could ask for time off to accompany me on a once-in-a-
lifetime work trip to Greece, where I was speaking at the inaugural Women
Empowerment Awards in Athens. In addition to the week off in July, she
also wanted to end her internship a week early to travel with friends.

She was anxious about making the ask, so together we planned how
she would do it. She created a mini business case, reasoning that she was
one of the few interns who had worked for the company the entire spring
leading up to the summer role and therefore had earned some additional
time off. She offered to start her job a week early to make up for ending
early. She explained the reason for wanting to join me—to get exposure to
the international business world. All of this was done via Slack, the online
messaging platform, instead of with live human interaction, so when her
millennial boss responded with short and noncommittal answers, like a
thumb's up emoji, she assumed all was going to be fine.

Later that day, she called me, crying. Her boss had reported her requests
to the college internship organizer for breaking the rules by asking for time
off in the middle of the 10-week program. She was devastated when the

administrator requested to meet with her personally and used her as an example for the rest of the interns of what not to do!

She was disappointed and embarrassed, so I encouraged her to communicate live—via voice, video, or in person—with both her boss and the intern administrator. There is too much misunderstanding over IM, text, or even email, and these important conversations require human connection, especially when the relationships are important. I also coached her to stay curious and seek to understand why her boss hadn't just picked up the phone to work it out with her and why the administrators felt she had broken the rules of the program.

A few days later, she called me back, acknowledging that she had inadvertently violated the terms of the agreement, but the boss had agreed with the program leaders that Madeleine had made a good case and allowed her to start her internship early and head to Greece with me. She got some of what she wanted, and we had a very special adventure together.

It's Never Too Late to Learn from Mistakes and Try Again

When we don't make the ask at all, either because we don't think we can or because we're too afraid to take the risk, we're likely to have some regret. But what about when we do make the ask and we are told no? And worse, what if it all goes wrong, and backlash or harmed relationships result from our ask? First, being told no isn't a failure—it plants the idea in someone's head, and they'll often respect you for asking and engaging with them in a positive way. Second, if things do go off the rails, it's never too late to acknowledge the tough lesson and try again a different way. Like my daughter realizing that sending important requests via IM may not be the best method, I have learned from some mistakes along the way.

In chapter three, I told the story of my 2021 performance review with three of my board members. We had just completed an exceptional year and achieved all our goals after several difficult years. I was looking forward to the conversation and had prepared a detailed document on my perspective of my performance, including business objectives, leadership strengths, and opportunities to improve in the coming year. Instead of leading the conversation, I assumed the executives had read my document, so I asked for their comments. To save time, the board chair dove right in and began highlighting the two weaknesses they thought I could improve upon. I was blindsided and felt punished, and I reacted with anger.

That moment was *not* the time to make an ask, as my Inner Critic had spiked to One Up, but I couldn't help myself. With my performance review complete, I shifted the conversation to what I and the executive team needed from them to continue our transformation progress and prepare the company for sale. These were big asks around compensation packages and employment contracts. Now *they* were blindsided and angry. It was the first serious disagreement I'd ever had with my board, and we ended the call abruptly.

Before the meeting, I had planned and practiced with my CEO coach how I would separate the performance conversation from the executive team compensation negotiation, given that both deserved special attention. But because the performance conversation was so short and I was reacting emotionally to their criticisms, I made a critical mistake by diving right into my requests. After the call, my Inner Critic bounced to One Down: *Look what you've done—you ruined your chance to advocate for yourself and the executive team! You've lost the trust of the board! You're an ineffective CEO!* After a few days had passed and I returned to Compassionate Center, I crafted the email articulating the handful of levers we could use to incentivize the team and me, along with my recommendation of what I felt we needed to do to move forward.

It's critical to know that I did not send that email right away. Instead, based on guidance from some trusted advisors, I got very grounded, set the intention for a meaningful connection and productive conversation with my board chair, and picked up the phone. I calmly talked through every point in the email, starting with the acknowledgment of the misstep I had made. He expressed his gratitude for the call and promised to consider all my requests with the other board members. I sent the email afterward to confirm the details of our conversation, and within a week, we had worked out mutually agreeable terms, which resulted in about 80 percent of what I had hoped for. It was a painful lesson about when and how to make an important ask, but I declared victory and moved on.

The most important point here is to start asking, even if you make mistakes and have to try again. Think about your clarity statement. What do you want or need to get closer to the life you envision? That intention is stronger than the fear of asking, and it can propel you forward. Here are a few steps to help you get stronger at making the ask.

ACT NOW
How to Make the Ask

Think about a specific ask you want right now, one that would take you a step closer to what you envisioned in chapter five on Clarity.

1. **Clarify what you want and the "why" behind it.** Prepare yourself for the ask by determining exactly what you are asking for. Be as specific and concrete as possible. It often helps if you include the "why" behind your ask when you're making it, giving the context of the ask so the other person can fully understand. Here's an example:

    * What do I want? To reduce the number of my direct reports but not change my pay or level.

    * Why? I have too many direct reports to give each of them enough attention or support, and there are people on the team who need more experience with management. I recommend creating an additional management tier to allow others on the team to take on some of that responsibility.

2. **Quantify the value you bring.** This can be quantitative or qualitative, but articulating your personal value to the person you are asking can help them understand why you deserve what you are asking for. Collect data to be more persuasive:

   ✳ I talked to HR to understand the average number of direct reports of our managers, and I am over that threshold.

   ✳ I have thought through who on my team could be elevated to a manager and what the impact would be.

3. **Determine the right timing and the best medium for delivery.** Timing your ask is key to getting a yes:

   ✳ You don't want it to be in the middle of another discussion or to get lost in a larger conversation.

   ✳ Ask, "Is this a good time for my question?" as a good way to find a clear window and to alert the person that an ask is coming.

   ✳ For very important asks, and for anyone in Generation X or older, it is important to be "live" when making your ask, via voice, video, or in person. For less important asks, and for millennials or Gen Z, it might be okay to opt for email, text, or IM. But be aware of the risks given the lack of context, tone, or body language in those mediums.

4. **Use the three Ps to deliver the ask.** The three Ps (Point, Proof, Possibility) are a simple framework to support you through this process, which includes creating specific talking points. See how the example above could play out in the delivery:

   (Point) From my view, the number of direct reports I have is too high. My goal is to continue to be an effective and impactful manager. (Proof) Based on that goal, I collected data from both HBS and SHRM that shows managers shouldn't have more than seven to nine direct reports. I also asked our HR to let me know the average number of direct reports in our business unit, which is seven. (Possibility) I recommend moving both Shirley and Omar to report into Jane, which gives Jane more management experience.

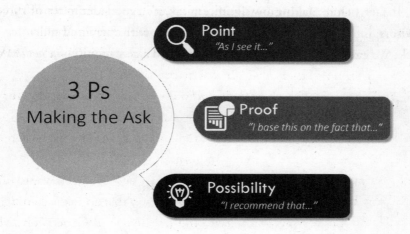

I also recommend a fourth P—Practice! For very important asks, you should practice as much as you can with different people. This gives you an opportunity to become comfortable with the language of the three Ps and get feedback on the ask itself. Is the ask clear? Are my business case and data sound? What questions should I be prepared to answer? These will all help you get ready for the ask.

Be prepared for the likely objections of the recipient. Brainstorm in advance how you might overcome them. This will help you be ready in the moment with clear, concise, and effective responses.

More importantly, know how you are going to react to a no. Have some questions ready to confirm whether this is a solid no, a "not right now," or something you can negotiate. You won't get a yes on every ask, and that's okay. Keep asking, and you'll be amazed at how far you will get.

As I enter the fourth decade of my career, I have had a lot of experience and practice with making the ask. But regardless of how high in organizations we rise, this hurdle is one that continues to be critical to achieving what we want in our career and entire life. This hurdle and the last—Networking—are two that continue to be central to ongoing success and fulfillment.

In fact, before making any significant ask, it's a good idea to consult your advisors, internally or externally, to test the ask with them and solicit feedback. We can't evolve as leaders alone. We need a community—a network.

10

Networking—Build Relationships That Make You Stronger

RATE YOURSELF (1–5)

In day-to-day work as a leader, I . . .					
Actively establish and leverage a broad network of relationships inside and outside the organization.					
Rarely Demonstrate 1	Sometimes Demonstrate 2	Often Demonstrate 3	Very Often Demonstrate 4	Almost Always Demonstrate 5	N/A
○	○	○	○	○	○

I was fortunate to discover the benefits of networking at a very young age. My parents were schoolteachers in Germany, where I grew up. Later, my father became an entrepreneur and pursued many endeavors, from Scherer Tours in Europe—where my brother and I played in his tennis camps all summer and skied all winter—to importing wine and cars from Europe to Florida, where we moved when I was 12. He ended his career selling insurance.

While my dad's entrepreneurial life was exciting and rewarding in many ways and surely influenced my own journey, at times there were cash-flow issues. When I needed money for hip jeans or a homecoming dress, I was on my own to find a job and earn it. By the time I was 15, I was already a hustler, so I pursued my first real summer job the only way I could imagine—I filled out applications and went from restaurant to restaurant until I was hired. While this was a valuable experience, it was the only job I ever got that didn't hinge on networking.

A few years later, when I was 17, my father helped me get a professional job through his friend Diego, who ran a successful stock brokerage business. Once I got in and proved myself, I spent the next three summers working there with increasing responsibility—first as the receptionist, then administering new accounts, and then leading their marketing efforts. The connections I made helped me with future roles, and for many years I kept in touch with the fun clan at International Assets Advisory Corp. They became an early foundation of my network, and I recognize how important those early experiences were. I used those connections for references and investment advice for several years.

Now, several decades later, I encourage women to take the time to broaden and leverage their networks. They often acknowledge the need for networking but don't really know where to start and are reticent to act. While a strong network is vital to career progression, building and activating a network can feel daunting. There are multiple studies that demonstrate women's networks are less powerful than men's, and women are less able to use the networks they have. These are challenges we can fix.

What's more, the younger we start networking, the better. I saw the power of networking early on in my career and want to ensure women don't wait to discover it until much later. It takes time, but networks build on top of each other, and early efforts are bound to pay off eventually.

WHAT IS NETWORKING, EXACTLY?

At its foundation, networking is about actively establishing and leveraging a broad spectrum of relationships inside and outside your organization. It helps us stay connected to what is happening in the world in those areas most important to us and in turn helps connect the world to us. It's a reciprocal give-and-take that unfolds over time (you "give" more at certain points in the relationship and "take" more at others), and it is essential for leadership and advancement.

It's also important to clear up some misconceptions about networking. For instance, traditionally we've viewed networking much like a blind date before dating apps: face-to-face, uncomfortable, and often wrongly matched. Another misconception is that networking is for extroverts, and introverts can't or won't do it. In fact, technology evolution over the last 20 years has created a much more even playing field where networking doesn't happen primarily at conferences or on the golf course. It's now easier to connect online. Finally, we need to dispel the notion that a bigger network is a better network. Sending out mass emails or accepting every LinkedIn invitation won't necessarily build a strong or effective network, but it will waste a lot of time.

It's true that networking can be overwhelming, which is why we need clarity to focus our efforts. For example, as a CEO in the mid-market leadership space, I prioritize my networking by connecting with current or potential advisors, partners, customers, and even competitors—people with whom I can give and receive specific help on my and their personal and organizational goals. Over the course of my career, networking has continued to rise in importance at every stage. Every single job I have ever landed has been the result of leveraging my network versus being "discovered" or throwing my résumé into a deep, dark hole.

WHY IS NETWORKING A HURDLE FOR WOMEN?

There are many theories about why women struggle with networking, the most common being that women don't prioritize it, are uncomfortable investing time in it, or aren't included in the activities where networking among men has traditionally flourished—at sporting events, the bar, or the golf course. An interesting research study published in *Forbes* offers six obstacles that explain why women struggle to overcome this networking hurdle, and some are surprising:[1]

* Women tend to prefer networking with lower-level employees and peers.
* We lack the confidence that we can make valuable contributions to our networks.
* We perceive networking as disingenuous and exploitative self-advancement instead of as building authentic, collaborative relationships.
* Childcare issues keep women from attending evening or weekend events.
* We feel excluded from "male bonding" activities where networking often takes place.
* In general, people (both men and women) prefer networking with others like themselves. Obviously, this makes it harder for women to break into male-dominated networks.

While there are no quick and easy solutions to these obstacles, being aware that these roadblocks exist is the critical first step to overcoming them. We might have to shift our thinking, move out of our comfort zone, and experiment with new approaches, but these are not insurmountable obstacles.

Intentionally curating a network is only one side of the challenge. The other, even harder part is activating the network by regularly nurturing and leveraging the power of the connections you've built. This is where Making the Ask comes in—being bold and requesting time, information, an introduction, or advice from your network. Women have an easy time offering to help those in our network who ask, but we don't believe that the same help will be given freely to us when we need it. We have concerns about using social ties for personal gain and ensuring there is equilibrium in the asking and offering.

These are internal biases, and we need to explore and overcome them because if we can, our efforts will unlock a world of possibility. Making an investment in relationships will provide mutually beneficial outcomes over time, far greater than anything we can do alone.

WHAT HAS CHANGED IN THE LAST FEW YEARS?

Due to the disruption of COVID-19, networking has shifted significantly from traditional in-person events, often held in a big noisy room, to a largely virtual environment. Besides the benefit of highly targeted selection and messaging (far more effective than a broad, scattered approach), this shift has made networking more casual and natural. This bodes well for women—a specific and thoughtful ask on LinkedIn to a new contact is far easier and more comfortable for many of us than approaching them in person. If we feel excluded or intimidated in most business networking environments where we are vastly outnumbered by men, virtual engagement can level the playing field.

But more than just *how* we network, massive changes are impacting *why* we network and *with whom*. The world is becoming far more complex, with new leadership issues to navigate related to technology, hybrid work, economic uncertainty, and the political and cultural landscapes. While networking inside our own organization is important, we also need a strategic network that helps us connect with people and conversations beyond those walls and brings us new information and opportunity. I often use my external network to compare what we're doing with what we're seeing in the larger environment, including the competitive pressures and best practices.

NETWORKING IN REAL LIFE

One of my biggest discoveries when I started my first CEO role in 2018 was the importance of carefully selecting, engaging, and nurturing critical trusted advisors in my network. This was the year during which, after more than 20 years in the leadership industry, I had taken a self-defined sabbatical to help define exactly what I wanted out of my next role, as I discussed in chapter five on Clarity. During this time, I actively pursued and relied on an informal advisory board to help me weigh job opportunities against my personal purpose and vision.

I knew I wanted to continue to lead, manage, and grow businesses in the leadership space. But there were many ways to do that: through publicly traded companies, startup ventures, and established medium-sized organizations. So, I actively pursued all three, relying on different members of my network to broker introductions for me to new people who could help me narrow my decision about which path I wanted to pursue. I made a list of people by category and contacted them via email or LinkedIn to ask for advice and support.

Over time, this approach provided a clear path to what would be most meaningful at this stage in my career: a midsize company where I could be a C-level leader, ideally a CEO. I called on a subset of my advisors to learn more about the private equity markets and another to help me navigate the terms of job opportunities.

Through this process, I learned the priceless value of the network I had built over decades and now relied on throughout my transition. For the first time in my life, I truly embraced and enjoyed a pause in my career, confident that the perfect role would emerge because I had clarified my intention and put a plan in motion, with a circle of advisors supporting me. In this stage, I spent more time asking for help, knowing that there would be other times when the situation would reverse and I would be doing more giving. As mentioned earlier, the exchange isn't always even, but over time there should be a natural flow of give-and-take.

When I started my role as Linkage CEO, I spent several months engaging our board of directors, executive team, clients, partners, and vendors. Slowly, I developed an expanded set of trusted advisors, whom I informally call my "CEO Success Circle." They play specific roles in my circle of trust because I know I can't do it alone. Some are fellow CEOs who can commiserate with me about the challenges (and sometimes loneliness) of the role. Others are thought partners who can guide me in specific areas I've not led before. Others are coaches who can hold a mirror up to my own leadership behavior and gently steer me.

I have learned that actively managing this group of partners is a significant investment of time and energy, but it is a critical part of my job, and it is exceptionally rewarding work.

Building Your Network Strategically Can Change Your Life

The latest inductee to my CEO Success Circle is Alan Mulally, the former CEO of the Ford Motor Company and Boeing Commercial Airplanes. He has changed my life and my career thanks to an impulsive ask I made when I first met him in 2020 after an early-morning workout in a San Diego hotel gym.

In January of that year, just weeks before COVID-19 shut down the entire world, I had the incredible privilege to be at the annual gathering of the Marshall Goldsmith 100 Coaches, a group of some of the world's most influential management thinkers, iconic leaders, academics, coaches, and advisors. I had been nominated to the organization a few months before, and I sat at a table right up front to immerse myself in the interactive workshop that Marshall led with Alan. It was designed to teach us how Alan had led and transformed two American icons—the Boeing Company[2] and the Ford Motor Company[3]—through two of the biggest crises in US history: 9/11 and the Great Recession of 2008–09.

As I heard Alan speak about his life as a CEO, I couldn't stop thinking about how what he had done could apply to my own leadership, executive team, and organization. I wanted to learn more. The next morning, jet-lagged and on East Coast time, I woke up at 5 AM and hit the gym tread-mill with my iPad in hand, reading article after article about Alan and his "Working Together Leadership and Management System and Culture of Love by Design."[4]

I was fascinated by the weekly structure Alan had put in place called the Business Plan Review (BPR) to ensure everyone was focused and aligned on the company goals and aware of how the team was progressing. Every business metric would be coded red, yellow, or green, which allowed everyone to quickly determine what areas needed to be swarmed with special attention.

Immediately, I knew I wanted to borrow this system but didn't know how to take the next step without Alan's guidance. I finished my workout, and, still sweaty in my gym clothes, I dropped by the hotel executive club lounge on the upper floor of the Hyatt Regency to grab some fruit and coffee.

And there Alan was, waiting by the toaster. By himself.

I watched him for a minute, summoning up the courage and the words to address him. I knew I only had one chance to make the ask, and I took it.

"Excuse me, Alan. I was in the front row all day yesterday. I'm the CEO of Linkage, a private equity–backed leadership development firm, and I've been struggling to get our team aligned on our vision and our plan to exe-cute it. I know your 'Working Together' system with its BPR process would help our company, but I don't know how to take the next steps. Would you help me?"

That single conversation led to Alan taking me on as a protégé and began a meaningful relationship with one of the greatest leaders of this century. During the initial panic of 2020, he counseled me on how to use

"Working Together" to unite our workforce quickly and focus on the most critical action items. It was the hardest year of my entire career, and we had to make devastating decisions that impacted our staff, clients, vendors, and partners. But the executive team was transparent, honest, and fair, and even though our company was in a free fall like so many others that year, I believe Alan and his "Working Together" strategy helped Linkage recover and prosper. In many ways, we emerged even stronger, accelerating our innovation and transformation strategy during those pandemic years.

Alan was there alongside me whenever I asked for his help. He believed in our mission and was invested in me and the success of Linkage. He led a free webinar with me for thousands of leaders globally who were struggling to navigate the crisis. He accepted our Linkage Legend in Leadership Award and recorded an inspiring fireside chat with me that aired for the nearly 1,400 women at our first-ever virtual Women in Leadership Institute™ in 2020. And in 2022, Alan joined me virtually at our first staff retreat in 28 months, helping our entire organization develop a greater understanding and appreciation for the Linkage "Working Together" practices he helped us instill.

When you establish a connection with someone, it's important to maintain that relationship and not let it drift away. There is a good balance to strike between keeping in touch and becoming overwhelming, and I try to always offer something in my outreach.

Spend More Time Preparing than Engaging Your Network

I spend most of my time with Alan on Zoom or FaceTime listening and learning, but I spend twice as much time preparing for my time with him or following up after our conversations. When I have an offer or a request, I carefully craft my email outreach to him before and after our interactions.

With Alan's permission, I offer a few excerpts from our emails here to give examples of how to keep communication open and nurture the relationship.

From: Jennifer McCollum
Date: Thursday, May 5, 2022 at 8:42 AM
To: Alan Mulally
Subject: Invitation to inspire our team on June 8

Dear Alan,
I hope you'll consider inspiring our Linkage team for 30 mins on
June 8 in Boston (you of course could dial in virtually). From June
7–9, our staff will meet in person for the first time in more than two
years. For the all-staff portion of our retreat on June 8, we will offer
the team our work in progress on our 2023–25 strategic plan and
seek their input. We'll also celebrate the culture we have created,
and any evolution needed in our Working Together principles to
ensure we hit our plan (or create a better plan). We need to help
the team understand the critical meaning behind "profitable growth
for all." Performance creates opportunity for all our stakeholders,
including our employees, investors, and clients.

From: Alan Mulally
Date: Saturday, May 7, 2022 at 7:51 PM
To: Jennifer McCollum
Subject: Re: Invitation to inspire our team on June 8

Hi Jennifer!
Pleased to support you!
:)))
Alan

From: Jennifer McCollum
Date: Friday, July 1, 2022 at 9:43 AM
To: Alan Mulally

Cc: Sarah McArthur
Subject: Working Together Always Works: A Linkage Update

Alan,

As we delivered our fireside chat to the Linkage staff just over three weeks ago, I couldn't see our way to our second-quarter sales and revenue goals, which I knew would put the company sale and valuation at significant risk. We had been completely open about our uphill climb but always believed in our ability to achieve our aspiration. In reflecting now on our first-half results, I am amazed at what we achieved in June, fueled greatly by your impact on me and our Linkage team, combined with my trust in "Working Together."

I'm happy to report that we closed the quarter 97% to goal, with the largest month in Linkage sales in the last 5 years. We've grown 21% year over year, on top of 30% growth in 2021. It feels good, and the staff is celebrating wildly.

Working together always works.

On another note, you asked about the feedback from our session. So many employees commented to me personally how much they enjoyed your presentation and how inspired and thankful they were to hear from you directly. It really helped cement for them the background on the principles and practices we use ourselves every week in our own BPR meetings and especially the value of the Special Attention Meetings (SAMs). The amazing Kelly Gruber on my team aggregated all the offsite metrics and asked me to forward the highlights to you. I have the entire report but will share that only if you want it 😊.

Once again, I can't thank you and Sarah enough for the selfless commitment of your time and willingness to ensure our session was perfect, down to the Linkage logo and my signature on the slide. We are so grateful!

Please enjoy your July 4th holiday. I'm off to Greece today on business and taking my 20-year-old daughter, who will accompany me to a keynote on the state of women's leadership—and then a fun-filled few days in Santorini!
Jennifer

From: Alan Mulally
Date: Friday, July 1, 2022 at 1:14 PM
To: Jennifer McCollum
Cc: Sarah McArthur
Subject: Re: Working Together Always Works: A Linkage Update

Hi Jennifer!!
Wonderful to hear!!
    Working Together always works . . . with the leadership of a Working Together Leader!
    That would be You!!
    So pleased for and proud of your leadership and your team's success!
    Love to see the entire report . . . no hurry!
    Enjoy your special time with your daughter in Greece!
Thank you!
Alan

Ensure an Equal Exchange of Give-And-Take

In addition to preparing for networking conversations, it's important to maintain your network and ensure there is a balance of give-and-take. I am so grateful to Alan and his "Working Together" Leadership and Management System that I seek every opportunity to acknowledge and honor both. When I talk at conferences about the impact of Alan's leadership on Linkage and me, I often have people approach me to share the impact Alan has had on their lives. Every time, via a quick email or text, I relay it to Alan.

One participant at a Chamber of Commerce event in Maryland had owned a Ford dealership while Alan was CEO of Ford Motor Company. He told me how he was moved to tears when Alan instructed the Ford employees at a convention to share with their Ford dealers that they love them, because success was only possible with their leadership and "Working Together." I took a selfie of the man and me and texted it to Alan on the spot, thanking him for changing yet another life.

After our 2022 staff offsite, I posted on LinkedIn the leadership lessons Alan conveyed to our team during his virtual appearance, and nearly 3,000 people viewed the post. It allowed me an opportunity to expand the reach of what Alan had shared and engage other members of my network. Right away, I heard from Ted Johnson via LinkedIn messenger. He is a highly valued client who is also an avid fan of Alan's:

Tedrick Johnson • 7:24 PM

Ok, so...I try not to let envy seep in, but Alan is your mentor??? That's amazing!! I'm a lifetime Ford junkie, loyalist, and shareholder. He's incredible.

Hope you are well! As I write this, I'm in quarantine, CoVID+. Sigh....

It's still real. Stay safe.

Jennifer McCollum • 10:23 PM

YES! I was so fortunate to meet Alan in 2020, just before the pandemic. I'll send you the video fireside chat he did with our staff and me last week, you'll love him even more! I assume you've read American Icon?

And Covid? NOW? You've been through so much...there must be a higher plan. Stay strong, sending healing thoughts.

Jennifer

The exchange offered me an opportunity to reach back out to Alan to recognize him again and allowed me to give my client a gift—the link to the fireside chat of Alan and me, which he could watch as he recovered.

> **From:** Jennifer McCollum
> **Date:** Monday, June 13, 2022 at 11:12 AM
> **To:** Alan Mulally
> **Cc:** Sarah McArthur
> **Subject:** RE: Link to our magical performance last week
>
> In case you ever wondered if people wanted even MORE from you as one of our world's greatest leaders of the last century, the answer is YES!
>
> Ted Johnson is a large client of ours from HCA Healthcare, the national group VP of Physician Services. He is also an exceptional leader who sends inspiring emails weekly to his very large team (see latest attached). He reached out to me Sunday to tell me what a huge fan of yours he is . . . and sadly, his home just burned down and then he caught COVID. I sent him our video and encouraged him to watch it as he recovers.
>
> You are a gift to the world!
> Jennifer

Nurture the Long-Term Members of Your Network

While Alan is a more recent addition to my network across the last few years, Andrew has been a pivotal member for nearly 15 years. He was an executive and mentor at my former company CEB from 2009–13 and was instrumental a few years later when he helped me secure a job to help him lift a new business unit at a prestigious leadership company he had recently joined.

While the job didn't last there, my connection with Andrew did, and he has played a critical role as an advisor to me, encouraging me to take the CEO job and using his experience and contacts to help guide my path. Here's an example of our engagement:

From: Jennifer McCollum
Date: March 21, 2018 at 1:38 PM
To: Andrew
Subject: Help—I got both job offers!

Andrew,

I got both offers—CEO at the PE-owned leadership company and the North America business unit leader at the global nonprofit! They are so different in terms of role, investor expectations, and compensation structure that I would really value 30 minutes of your time to help me think through the CEO offer especially. Given your current role as CEO of a PE portfolio, I know you'd have some great insight into what I could expect and negotiate in terms of a comp package. I also would value any lessons learned from the negotiation/contracting process.

Are you available at all in the next few days?
Kindly, Jennifer

From: Andrew
Date: March 21, 2018 at 7:14 PM
To: Jennifer McCollum
Subject: RE: Help—I got both job offers!

Yay—congratulations! I'm not surprised. I am in Asia but have a long layover on Friday night Asia time, Friday morning for you. Would be at about 9 AM Eastern. Any good? Send me an invite if so. Otherwise in SF next week.
Andrew

With Andrew, I try to do a semiannual check-in with him, with at least one in-person gathering each year. He is a seasoned CEO and one of my most valued sounding boards, and he has also become a friend. In addition to work, we talk about our kids, our health, and our future aspirations. Then, when something critical comes along, like the sale of our company, it is very natural that I would reach out to Andrew.

From: Jennifer McCollum
Date: Saturday, February 19, 2022 at 6:33 PM
To: Andrew
Subject: Going to Market

Andrew,
We're going to market with the company next week, which was our goal when I took this job! I'd like to get your thoughts on the process with the investment bank. It's go time, very exciting!
Jennifer

From: Andrew
Date: Sunday, February 20, 2022 at 9:26 AM
To: Jennifer McCollum
Subject: Re: Going to Market

Ping me if I can be a resource for you sooner and/or later. In the meantime, best of luck with the process. From my experience, it's a heady combo of exhaustion and exhilaration! The trick is to do all of that while continuing to run the business, and that's hard, but hitting numbers is a big part of a successful process in itself.
All the best.
Andrew

Don't Be Afraid to Leverage New Connections for an Immediate Purpose

When I brought my daughter on the business trip to Greece in July 2022, we took the opportunity to add a few days on the most beautiful Greek island, Santorini. While at a hotel-sponsored champagne tasting, we struck up a conversation with Pam and Burt from Florida, and our discussion naturally turned to what had brought us to Greece and my specific work on empowering women. Pam then told me about her friend who had written a book on the topic, and it didn't take me long to figure out it was Sheryl Sandberg, the outgoing COO of Meta (formerly Facebook).

Pam and her husband were going to Sheryl's wedding in Jackson Hole the following month. I knew Sheryl would be a perfect fit to speak on our stage at the Women in Leadership Institute™, so I asked if I could follow up with Pam, and we exchanged contact information. Later that night, I explained to my daughter that Pam was now a part of my network, and it was up to me to follow up with her. Before going to bed, we texted Pam a photo of the evening and thanked her for the conversation and connections.

When I returned to the US the following week, I texted her again to ask if I could send her an email inviting Sheryl to our conference. She responded right away and agreed.

From: Jennifer McCollum
Date: July 14, 2022 at 12:32 PM EDT
To: Pam
Subject: Invitation to honor Sheryl Sandberg as a Legend in Leadership (Nov 2022 or 2023)

Hello Pam,
Thank you so much for offering to connect me with Sheryl. I realize how busy she is, transitioning out of Meta and focusing on her wedding and future philanthropy, but I think the opportunity to honor her

as a "Legend in Leadership" would be mutually beneficial. If you're open to it, please pass along the email below.

Thanks so much, and I do hope we stay in touch!

Best, Jennifer

Pam forwarded the email to Sheryl right away, and within 48 hours, her communications manager, Brittany, responded with unfortunate news:

From: Brittany
Date: Monday, July 18, 2022 at 9:56 PM
To: Jennifer McCollum
Subject: Re: FW: Hi

Hi Jennifer, my name is Brittany, and I support communications at Sheryl Sandberg's foundation. It's nice to meet you!

Thank you for reaching out and thinking of Sheryl for this award and event opportunity! As you can imagine, Sheryl is inundated with event and speaking requests right now, and as much as she would like to accommodate them all, it's not possible given her work and family responsibilities.

We appreciate your understanding, and let me know if you have any questions.

Best,

Brittany

From: Jennifer McCollum
Date: Thursday, July 21, 2022 at 8:35 AM
To: Brittany
Cc: Katharine
Subject: Linkage Legend in Leadership Award, at the Women in Leadership Institute™

Brittany,

While we're sorry it won't work out for this year, **would she be able to join us in person next year to accept the award, which was previously given to Alan Mulally, former CEO of Ford & Boeing Commercial Airplanes?**

We will be in the same place—the Omni ChampionsGate outside of Orlando, FL. The session would be at **3–3:30 PM on Wednesday, November 14, 2023.** Please let me know if you need any more information to evaluate the possibility of Sheryl joining us in person to accept this prestigious award! I'm including details below and have copied our WIL executive director, Katharine Panessidi.

Thank you so much for the consideration.

Best,

Jennifer

While I didn't get what I wanted, I was able to make a specific ask and learn whom I needed to influence to reach Sheryl Sandberg. Had I not met Pam, I would not be connected to Brittany. By the way, I haven't given up on Sheryl engaging with Linkage and me sometime in the next few years. Networking is an investment that may not always pay off immediately, but it will pay off over time—even if it's in ways you never envisioned or expected.

Helping Each Other: Networking Redefined

Our rise in leadership is never a straight path, and it is never accomplished alone. We need others, and it is never too early (or too late) to curate and activate a network. Sometimes getting started is as simple as reaching out, proactively, to help someone who needs it.

In this chapter, I have mostly focused on networking in terms of Making the Ask. But I am also mindful of the other side of networking, which is looking for ways to help others even when they don't ask. In fact, I'd love to see a shift in how we think about networking—recognizing that, at its heart, networking is simply about helping each other, especially women helping other women.

Thankfully, there are fewer scenarios today when we are the "only" woman in the room, but I am still one of the few female executives in most business settings. I have grown accustomed to it over time, but it is never easy. And what I've learned is that there is something powerful in banding together as a pack to help each other navigate what can be uncomfortable situations.

While in Greece, I invited my daughter to join me as I presented to a small group of CEOs and executives. As they arrived one by one, I introduced myself, and they naturally started engaging each other. The first eight or so were all men. Then, the first woman arrived. She was a seasoned leader, but from her body language and her introduction to me, I noted she did not have the title, scope, or influence that the rest did. She looked around nervously trying to find her way, and I approached her, eager to engage with her and learn more about her work, leadership aspirations, and challenges. When I excused myself to meet other guests, however, my daughter noticed that this woman left for the bathroom until the presentation started. Maybe it all just felt too hard.

That's one reason I'm so grateful for our Women in Leadership Institute™. With thousands of women together from across industries in an in-person and virtual environment, networking feels natural. We are there to help and support each other in our ongoing development and success. When men attend the Institute, usually in our Executive Sponsor track, they report being overwhelmed by the feeling of being the minority. I recently learned from a former client that several years back, he had asked one of his male leaders to attend our conference as a participant. The man skipped a dinner event because it was too hard for him to be the "only."

That irony is not lost on women who have spent most of their careers as the "only" or the "few."

Out in the wild, away from supportive conferences, we women need to stick together. Women historically have not helped each other, due in part to the real bias and fear that there wasn't enough room at the top for more than one woman. That is no longer the case, and just as men have taken advantage of deep networks for centuries, women now have strength and power in greater numbers than ever before. We need to help each other rise.

Eisha Armstrong is a great example. She is the founder and CEO of Vecteris, an organization designed to help services companies transform their organizations by creating scalable and repeatable products. Kristen Howe and I were important members of Eisha's network when she launched her company in 2018, and we have supported her success ever since. We hired her and her talented team to help us with several Linkage projects, swarmed her with references for other potential clients, and offered her our own counsel and experience as fellow executives in a larger organization. I now serve on the Vecteris advisory board and have introduced Eisha to our private equity investors with the hope of expanding her reach to other small- and mid-market portfolio companies. I look forward to supporting her through the next phase of growth as she considers an external capital infusion and an eventual sale. We all win when women business owners and executives succeed.

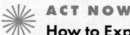

ACT NOW
How to Expand and Manage Your Network

Expanding Your Network

As we build our networks, we tend to seek out people who are like us in terms of values, level, role, industry, age, gender, education, race, etc. Just as we've become more aware of the need for diversity and inclusion in our workplaces, our networks should follow suit. Set the intention to go outside your comfort zone and broaden your network by including people who are different from you. Consider these tips as you reenergize your networking efforts:

1. Every day is an opportunity—if you haven't invested enough time in your network up to this point, today is a perfect time to start.

2. Based on your clarity statement, identify three to five people, internally or externally, who might be able to help you achieve your aspiration. Do the same in reverse—who are the three to five people you might be able to help?

3. Consider inbound networking requests carefully, even if you don't know why someone wants to connect with you. Take a minute to investigate the contact and agree to a short meeting if appropriate. Nothing may come out of it, but that's okay!

4. Make a clear ask for networking. As you connect with people, explain why you want to connect, what you hope to get out of it, and why you think it could be mutually beneficial.

5. If someone says no to or ignores your request to connect, don't let it slow you down. People are busy and don't always respond. Keep going—someone else is out there who will say yes!

Prioritizing Your Network

Most of us have stagnant networks that were created accidentally because we happened to work with those people or have accepted connections reactively. Herminia Ibarra is a professor of organizational behavior at the London Business School and one of the top management thinkers in the world. She is an expert on the topic of networks and breaks them down into three categories: operational (for managing internal responsibilities), personal (for professional development), and strategic (for new business directions that can help you envision the future).

Women, Ibarra says, struggle more than men with strategic networking. That's why we need to take stock of who is already in our network as well as who is *not* but should be. Cultivating new contacts and keeping existing ones fresh is important, especially those in your strategic network who can help you achieve your future goals.[5]

1. **Who is in your network?** Analyze your network using Ibarra's three categories—operational, personal, and strategic—and decide whom you need to add to your network. Determine which categories make the most sense for your role, your clarity, and your aspirations. Use the list below to consider who isn't in your network that would benefit you. Consider both the quality and the quantity of your network.
   * Senior executive in your organization
   * Sponsor
   * Partner
   * Mentor
   * Coach
   * Connector
   * Industry insider
   * Idealist
   * Realist

2. **Who should be in your network?** Once you know the gaps in your network, create a plan to fill those gaps. Think big—who is the most senior person you can reach who might be able to help you? Here are some ideas to guide your planning:
   * Schedule a meeting with your boss's boss
   * Use your favorite networking platform to find:
      * An expert in a field you would like to know more about
      * An expert in your own field
      * Someone who has the job you are aspiring to, either inside or outside of your organization

   *   Craft a personal email to invite each person into a networking conversation

3. **Prepare for your networking conversation.** These conversations are about connecting with others. You should have an agenda, but you may not have a clear next step before you meet with them. There doesn't have to be an immediate action item—it may take months for your conversation to pay off. Determine a good schedule for talking again.

    Remember, there is rarely an equal balance between the giving and receiving from a network contact at any one moment, but there should be a balance across the course of time. Try not to be a scorekeeper; most imbalances work themselves out. Always err toward generosity with your time and effort, as that energy will more likely be returned.

* * *

In the next chapter, we'll move from addressing the individual hurdles women face to addressing how organizations—and men, specifically—can support women in overcoming the hurdles and advancing more quickly. For women, being aware of how others can help is important as you consider the environment you want to work in and whom to engage in your network to help you achieve your aspirations.

Consider sharing this book with your leaders so they can build their own awareness and understanding of the unique hurdles women face—but also so they can influence their organizations to evolve their culture, people systems and processes, executive commitment, and leadership development in ways that support all women rising alongside you and behind you.

Think of this as a call to action for both women and organizations—we need to do this together.

PART THREE

Eliminating the Hurdles

11

Choose an Organization Where Women Can Rise

So far in this book, I have mostly addressed individual women who are on the path to higher leadership roles. Now I'd like to switch gears. While I'm still speaking to these women, I am also speaking to the executives who make the decisions that determine how well our companies prioritize and commit to encouraging, supporting, and advancing the women in their leadership pipelines.

Here's a hard truth: women can do our part in overcoming the hurdles to advancement, but we can't do it alone. Our organizations need to evolve alongside us. Growth is much easier—and a whole lot more fun—when we are part of an organization where we feel we can thrive, where the conditions are supportive, and where it feels like our uniqueness is honored and we belong.

It may sound like a lot to ask, especially when awareness of these issues and opportunities has surged only in the last decade or so. But women are increasingly seeking and expecting these types of environments and no longer willing to wait for the slow pace of change that has already dragged on for too many generations. With fierce competition for strong female leaders, it is time for organizations to rise to the challenge or risk losing the talent war.

Linkage's research demonstrates that women leaders perform better, stay at their companies longer, and advance in their careers when organizations address four strategic dimensions: Culture, People Systems & Processes, Executive Action, and Leadership Development for Women.[1]

These are the specific areas that we recommend women evaluate when considering their future in their current organization or when looking for a new role. The purpose of this chapter is twofold: to guide women leaders as they navigate their careers *and* to guide executives in positions of power and influence to create the conditions that help women thrive.

Starting in 2016, we asked more than 16,000 women to share their perception of the places they work, aligned to the four dimensions in our strategic framework.

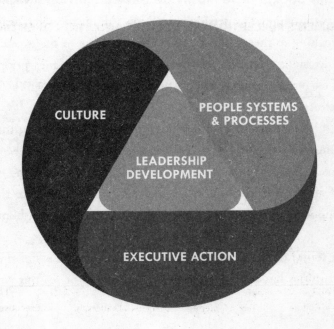

What we've learned across the last five years is fascinating. From 2017 to 2020, all four categories increased in their favorability ratings, meaning that organizations were making some good headway and progressing in their efforts to support women. We were initially surprised that scores continued to go up in 2020, given the panic and chaos of the first full year of the COVID-19 crisis and its detrimental impacts on women. However, we know that the women who took this survey—who are primarily college educated—stayed in their roles and went into survival mode, literally and figuratively. The workplace was their home, and, by and large, their organizations helped them stay afloat. That year, women were less worried about getting promoted or being tapped for a stretch experience; they just wanted a place where the culture and executives were understanding of the extreme challenges they faced.

Then came 2021, when we saw a sharp decline across every leading indicator we measure. This caused us some alarm at first. However, we realized it coincided with women beginning to leave their current roles in droves, dubbed the "Great Resignation" (though I prefer the other nicknames for

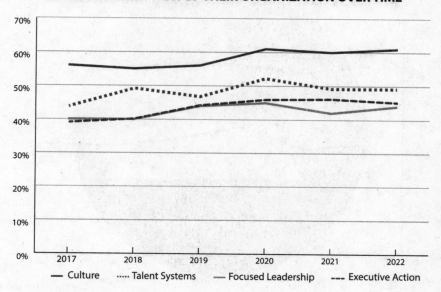

WOMEN'S PERCEPTION OF THEIR ORGANIZATION OVER TIME

— Culture   ..... Talent Systems   — Focused Leadership   ---- Executive Action that period, the "Great Awakening" or the "Great Reimagining," which are much more positive). The exodus sent shockwaves through the corporate world, but we weren't surprised at Linkage, because we were seeing the trends in our survey data.

In our survey, we also ask women four critical questions that give us leading indicators of their workplace perception:

* **Organizational Values Fit:** To what extent are the values of this organization a good fit with your own?
* **Organizational Engagement:** To what extent does this organization make it possible for you to directly contribute to its success?
* **Organizational Commitment:** If in the next two years you are offered the same or a similar job at another organization, how likely are you to make the move?
* **Net Promoter Score (NPS):** How likely is it that you would recommend this organization to a friend or colleague as a great place for women leaders to work?

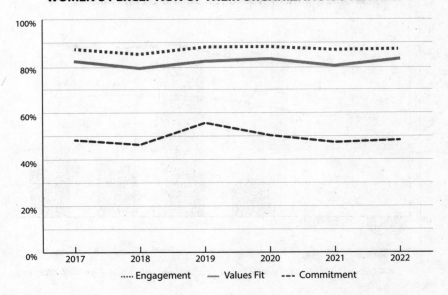

WOMEN'S PERCEPTION OF THEIR ORGANIZATION OVER TIME

With these questions, we also saw every score drop in 2021 but begin to rebound slightly in 2022. Women's engagement and values alignment, however, stayed relatively high across all years, while their commitment stayed low—less than half of women would stay at their organizations if offered a similar job elsewhere.

Most concerning, however, was the Net Promoter Score question. This number is derived by averaging the "promoters" (those who would recommend their organization) from the "detractors" (those who would not) and the "passives" (those who fall in the middle).

In 2021, the number of detractors rose significantly, while the number of promoters plummeted, which drove a steep decline in the overall NPS. While a "good" NPS score is considered around 30, on a scale from -100 to 100, this number peaked in 2020 at 17, telling us that while we were making progress, the overall average across the last five years was still low. But it was a shock to see the number fall in 2021 all the way down to 6, telling us that things were getting suddenly worse for women. In 2022, it rebounded slightly to 8, a number hardly worth celebrating.

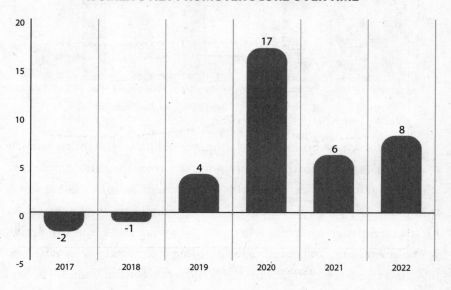

WOMEN'S NET PROMOTER SCORE OVER TIME

Even more interesting, when we looked at NPS by level, the director-level women—those in the pipeline to become the next executives—had the most detractors and the lowest NPS score by far, with a score of zero. This is consistent with the latest 2022 McKinsey and Lean In Women in the Workplace report[2] that showed women—especially those who are primed to become the most senior and have been the most burdened these last several years—aren't breaking up with work itself; they are breaking up with their companies to find something better. They reported that for every one woman promoted to VP, two directors leave.

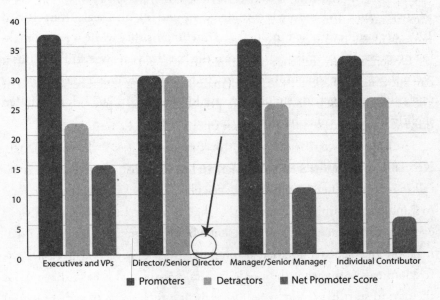

NET PROMOTER SCORE ACROSS ALL LEVELS

With those insights as the backdrop, we feel it's important for women to do their research on the organizations and roles they are considering, whether internally or externally, by asking questions and seeking input from other women to get a better understanding of the environment. As for the executives reading this book, it's up to you to gather this data inside your own company and examine these leading indicators to determine how likely it is that you will be able to attract and retain women leaders. The best organizations recognize the tremendous opportunity in creating and sustaining a positive environment—one that maximizes the collective intelligence and goodwill of all their people.

Let's review the four key dimensions individually.

CULTURE: DO WOMEN FEEL VALUED AND RESPECTED IN MY ORGANIZATION?

A shift toward a positive and inclusive culture can be more influential than strategy or policy, as it sends and reinforces messages about what is expected of employees—and what is valued and celebrated in the organization. Most importantly, culture can empower women leaders to make greater contributions to the business.

When women feel they are valued for the uniqueness they bring and can show up authentically at work, there is a freedom and acceptance that allows them to step into their true power. In these types of cultures, we don't feel we need to hide any aspect of ourselves to belong.

At Linkage, we strive to create this kind of culture. At the end of 2020, Kristen Howe approached me and relayed that she had breast cancer. After talking through her prognosis and her plan, I asked her how she wanted to handle communicating this news. She immediately responded, "I want everyone at Linkage to know." She sent a beautiful email to the entire organization and kept us updated throughout the journey. That gave her the freedom to ask for what she needed: to take dedicated breaks throughout the day, to start her workday at 10 AM during the month of radiation, and to continue including her in all the work because it would distract her and keep her going.

For our long-standing clients, we track their data over time to determine the return on their investment for their efforts to advance women. When we look at the culture metrics for organizations that have committed to purposeful and ongoing efforts, we find they improve over time. Items we measure include whether women feel welcome and respected in the organization, whether the quality of an employee's work is valued more than the number of hours worked, and whether there are women in important and visible positions of leadership.

Constellation Brands is a Fortune 500 company that produces beer, wine, and spirits. For six straight years, they have invested purposefully in their women leaders with dedicated leadership development programs, clear executive sponsorship, and an employee resource group of 600 women that surfaces recommendations to the chief diversity officer. The language of the Inner Critic and seven hurdles permeates the organization, including with men who have become greater allies because of their increased understanding of the challenges women face. Based on their measurement of the trajectory of the women who have received dedicated leadership development, 80 percent have stayed at the organization and 75 percent have been promoted or taken on an expanded role within a year. We see that reflected in the culture scores, which continued to steadily increase through 2021 even as our normative database declined, and Constellation Brands ranks among the highest of all organizations we've measured. In fact, the company's culture scores increased on average by 19 percent across the last five years and outperformed the Linkage norm on average by 5 percent. Tracking the perception of culture over time is important because it gives organizations proof that their investments are working and helps to solidify a strategy for what may need to evolve to ensure that women feel a sense of belonging and believe in their future with the company. Conversely, nothing will send high-potential talent running for the door more than a culture that demoralizes and minimizes women.

PEOPLE SYSTEMS & PROCESSES: DO WOMEN IN MY ORGANIZATION HAVE EQUAL OPPORTUNITIES?

Effective organizations understand that an emphasis on opportunity—embedded in people systems and processes—provides an avenue for women leaders to advance. Opportunities come in the form of programs that identify and encourage women to take on leadership roles, as well as human resource policies around critical decisions like hiring, performance management, promotion, compensation, benefits, and flexible work. Creating equity and removing bias in these decisions can open the floodgates for women to enter and advance in an organization.

The COVID-19 pandemic helped challenge assumptions and transform perspectives about talent policies as the world saw that much of the professional workforce could do their jobs much more flexibly, away from the rigidity of fixed office hours and long commutes. Linkage had already been a flexible work environment for many years, but after working remotely during the pandemic and not coming together in person for more than two years, we chose to close our office completely and become a fully virtual organization. Other companies have chosen to designate select office days, usually three days a week, with some light guidelines for the acceptable days or the hours. All to say, most organizations have integrated at least some remote work into their policies, a benefit that helps attract and retain high-caliber women leaders. According to the 2022 Women in the Workplace report, "only 1 in 10 women wants to work mostly on-site, and many women point to remote and hybrid work options as one of their top reasons for joining or staying with an organization."[3] Not only does this provide more flexibility, but women working remotely or in a hybrid environment experience "fewer microaggressions and higher levels of psychological safety."

In addition to those focused on creating better HR policies, we work with many clients focused on creating better talent systems. In late 2021, a publicly traded insurance company with operations in 54 countries gathered their top 160 women executives at the senior VP level and above. I delivered an interactive virtual keynote on the state of women in the workforce: the trends we were seeing, the unique challenges women face (the hurdles), and how organizations could help women overcome them (the four dimensions). We created breakout rooms where groups of executive women could talk through a subset of the 20 questions that we measure in our organizational assessment. This exercise was designed to give them a snapshot of where the company had strengths and where it had opportunity as an organization to further support its women leaders.

In just 90 minutes, the HR executives had overwhelming input on where the women thought the company could improve. One area they surfaced as a priority was the company's talent systems, which had received some of the lowest scores in the assessment. Items we measure include whether women feel the organization has human resource practices like childcare and family medical leave, along with flexible work schedules and locations; whether women are as likely to be promoted as men; and whether people-related decision-making processes like performance management, promotion, and compensation are transparent and fair and provide equal opportunities to women.

Ideas poured in around offering family-friendly benefits and more transparency in open roles and promotions. That single event created the opportunity for deeper data gathering, so the HR leaders then deployed the full assessment and used the results to inform a strategy to engage, support, and retain their most senior women leaders. Within a few months, they had revised their family-leave policy based on feedback the women had offered.

We know from our research that organizations with strong people systems and processes have more effective women leaders. In short, they attract and retain the best. For top companies, it's not just about becoming an employer of choice—women leaders in the organization must see a real possibility for equitable career progression, as well as the integration of their work within the context of their broader life.

LEADERSHIP DEVELOPMENT: IS MY ORGANIZATION PROVIDING FOCUSED DEVELOPMENT FOR WOMEN?

In most corporate environments, the model of effective leadership—the "rules of the game" or expected behavior—has been defined by men for generations. Men have learned these rules through natural access to other male leaders in their networks who have coached, mentored, and sponsored them along the way. So, it's not surprising that the corporate status quo perpetuates the advancement of men. Women historically have not had this access. For women leaders to grow and advance, companies must differentially invest in leadership development for women above and beyond what is typical for all leaders.

This specific development should focus on key advancement competencies that support women in overcoming the hurdles and can come from a combination of formal programs and experiences, high-visibility stretch assignments, or feedback and coaching. Companies that get this development right will see increases in key leading indicators like women's engagement, an aspiration to lead, and belief in their future with the company.

The specific questions we ask in this category center on the availability of training to help women overcome biases and challenges in the workplace, consistency in receiving feedback and coaching to increase their impact, and programs that are specifically tailored to both the needs of the business and the needs of women leaders. Importantly, we also measure whether the organization encourages women to take on stretch experiences and take advantage of opportunities outside the organization to develop, network, and broaden their perspectives.

At Linkage, we have measured the outcomes of women's development, specifically of the nearly 18,000 alumnae of our Women in Leadership Institute™. In our latest survey covering the previous five years of attendees, we learned that this investment in women's leadership development contributed specific benefits to women leaders themselves. Of the women who attended:

* 89% took more time to define their strengths and talents as a leader
* 86% gained more self-confidence
* 76% received more frequent recognition for their contributions

But that's not all. The organizations that made the investment in their women leaders also experienced transformational impact on the very leading indicators that are most important. Of the women who attended:

* 82% report that they and their teams are outperforming the company average
* 75% are more engaged with their work
* 69% have more personal satisfaction with their work
* 67% are more likely to stay with the company

Lenovo is a Fortune 200 technology company with more than 82,000 employees globally. It is one of my favorite client stories, as the company has been bold and public in its goals to increase the diversity of its executive population by 2025, measured by both female representation as well as historically underrepresented ethnic and racial groups. For both groups, Lenovo invests annually in carefully designed development programs and measures success along the way. In particular, its women's leadership development program pairs women leaders with executive sponsors to support their advancement. The results have been exceptional, with a 100 percent retention rate of program participants, 80 percent of whom received promotions.

A unique strategy Lenovo initiated in 2020 was the concept of the Talent Team, which helps address the entire talent ecosystem. One of the biggest risks in a development program is when the leader returns to her workplace reality and nothing in the environment has changed—culture, opportunity, or executive-level commitment. It's disheartening to the leader who wants to test out her new skills or move into a new role. Talent Teams are a group of individuals with a vested interest in the leader's development and include an executive sponsor and an HR team member. After receiving clear guidance from the DEI leaders on key elements of inclusive leadership and their role in the process, the Talent Team gathers with the leader regularly to discuss her career ambitions and how they can support her.

I'm often asked why this differential investment for women is needed at all, when most organizations have some type of leadership development that cuts across all leaders at all levels. Organizational leaders may even cite fears of "excluding" men. My response, informed by our research, is twofold: First, focused leadership development efforts directly impact employee engagement and, by extension, retention. The more an organization supports and encourages women to take on growth opportunities, the higher the levels of engagement the women report. And second, when it comes to the advancement of women leaders, personal aspiration is vital, and leadership development has a direct impact on a woman's aspiration to advance. This is about a woman's ability to see a clear path forward, even if there isn't a critical mass of women who have come before her.

EXECUTIVE ACTION: ARE MY ORGANIZATION'S EXECUTIVES ENGAGED IN EFFORTS TO ADVANCE WOMEN?

For women leaders to fully engage and be inspired by a future vision that includes gender equality, action is what matters. They must look up and see executives in their organization not only talking about advancing women but also taking steps to do so. Executive engagement can include initiating sponsorship programs to increase visibility of rising female talent, ensuring gender equity and knowledge of the women in the organization's pipeline, and promoting creative initiatives to retain female talent. When executives act, organizations demonstrate that they are committed to advancing women as a strategic priority.

Many organizations focus on allyship, coaching, or mentorship, and while all those are important, the most critical support women need is sponsorship because that is what has historically been lacking.[4] There is a difference: Everyone can be an ally, and those with experience can be a coach or mentor. But to be a sponsor, you need power and influence.

Here's an analogy to help you distinguish them. Picture a door that you really want to get through and the key people you need to help you:

Ally: Your friend and supporter who will cheer you on and encourage you to get to the door. They'll say good things about you and build you up whether or not you're in the room.

"She deserves to get through the door; no one does it better than she does!"

Coach: Often a manager, helping you with your aspirations. A coach will ask you to describe the door, put a plan in place for how to get through it, and hold you accountable.

"Let's identify development areas that will help you get through the door and craft an action plan to keep you on track."

Mentor: Will explain how she walked through the door and point you in the right direction. She may even walk alongside you until you get there.

"Let me tell you the obstacles I faced on my path to the door and how I overcame them."

Sponsor: Has power, influence, and political capital. They will use it to fight for you behind the door, hold the door open, and pull you through. Once you get there, they will do what it takes to create the conditions for success.

"I will make the introductions and find the experiences you need to get to this door and beyond."

The reason sponsorship is so important is it creates the conditions for so many critical outcomes for women. Employees with sponsors are:

* 69% more likely to advance to a more senior position
* 62% more likely to receive feedback on their career goals
* 31% more likely to receive feedback on their leadership style
* 20% more likely to feel like they belong in the culture of their current work environment

We know that women tend to get less support than men, resulting in fewer promotions. Women also get less feedback, less advice from senior leaders, and less access to one-on-one workplace activities like mentoring. It goes back to external bias, where we naturally favor people like "us." In this case, the "us" is usually other white men. Formal sponsorship programs can help overcome that bias, while helping executives develop specific sponsorship capabilities. Here's what a good sponsor does:

1. **Commit** to developing their leader, either personally or by helping them network with others. This could include coaching and mentoring but also includes creating stretch opportunities, skip-level conversations, or job shadowing.

2. **Connect** the leader inside and outside the organization to aid in their development. Sponsors should consider their leader an extension of their brand and allow her to use their social currency.

3. **Believe** that their leader has the potential to rise to the next level in the organization. While you can mentor and coach others to help them in their career even if you're not convinced about their capacity to advance, sponsorship requires absolute belief in them to champion the leader to other executives and find them new growth opportunities.

4. **Promote** and advocate for their leader. This might mean leading her to a new position within the organization, appointing her to a special committee or project, or connecting her to another leader in their network who can help.

There's a two-way street associated with executive sponsorship. Women leaders who have a sponsor need to play an active role in delivering with excellence, cultivating the relationship, providing visibility about what is happening in the organization, and promoting the legacy and leadership of the sponsor.

I've had both mentors and sponsors, but I distinguish between them because we need both. Most have been either white men or white women who weren't a lot like me. The men almost always had spouses who stayed home and took care of the house and kids, allowing the men to work and travel without much restriction. The women either didn't have children or they had a spouse whose career was secondary to theirs. Even though we had different life realities, several executives have believed in me and helped open doors along the way.

One of my most important mentors and sponsors is Melody Jones. She was in a position of power at CEB when I was hired and warned me then: "This will be a very tough job for you. This is a new role, and no one really understands what you do, as we don't have learning design and delivery capability inside this organization. It won't be easy, but I will help you."

Two years later, she helped build the case for my promotion to managing director and later helped guide me gracefully to an exit when the company was bought. She has given my name to recruiters as a CEO candidate and has advised me for nearly 15 years on important career decisions. She has been so critical to my success that I asked her to be on our board of directors at Linkage.

Every time I have needed Melody's help, she has been there. She has supported me in significant challenges, like how to navigate a difficult political landscape or how to engage effectively with peers or executives outside my silo. That counsel, based on her vantage point from the executive seat, helped me thrive (and sometimes survive) in every role I've been in across my last three companies. I'm doubtful I would have reached this point in my career without her guidance.

We need more Melody Joneses in our organizations. Companies who foster these kinds of relationships at scale are well positioned to succeed in their sponsorship efforts. An auto parts retailer we've been working with since 2022 does this especially well. They initiated an extensive 18-month executive sponsorship and women's development program, designed to build a more diverse pipeline to the executive level. The program pairs the company's top 35 executives with its top 35 women of color.

The goal is to develop both underrepresented women (starting with Black women) *and* the sponsors who have been selected to support them (most of whom are white men). Sponsors get to broaden their leadership and develop the cultural fluency to deepen relationships with all types of leaders inside the company. The group of women, whom they call the "protégés," gain access, exposure, and insight into executive leadership capabilities, as well as development guided by Linkage's framework for mastering the Inner Critic and overcoming the hurdles to advancement that women face.

The CEO has said publicly that he believes this program will have substantial impact on the company's success in the future. It is inextricably linked with its business agenda and growth strategy, including how it will continue to differentiate itself by becoming more relevant to the customer base, consumers, and team members it serves. The company's goals include building a more inclusive environment where everyone feels respected and heard at all levels of the organization. That environment was on full display when the company launched the program with a keynote address that I delivered alongside the CEO. As we concluded, the video chat erupted with comments from both sponsors and protégés about how proud they were to work with a company making this type of investment.

This organization shows us what real commitment looks like. And it is not alone. Companies will increasingly focus on executive-level engagement as the benefits of sincere and intensive efforts like this one start to become more visible.

WHY WE NEED WHITE MEN TO ACCELERATE THE ADVANCEMENT OF WOMEN LEADERS

No matter what, we will struggle to accelerate women's advancement without men.

In early 2021, I met Dr. Tonya Matthews, who is the CEO of the International African American Museum and an accomplished Black woman in both academia and business. I asked her why, despite the indisputable business case for gender equity and diversity in leadership, the dismal leadership statistics show there has been so little change across the last several decades. She answered, "It's the invisible forces."

I was confused, so asked her to clarify. She said, "As long as the invisible forces holding things in place are stronger than the forces for change, no amount of objective business-case data will change the existing structures. This is the grounding impetus for my radical empathy strategies." To her, the answer is an appeal to the heart, to curiosity, and to human connection, especially when addressing the leadership majority—white men. She believes if those men in power can see their own personal, emotional, and professional gain in helping women and minorities rise into positions of power, then these invisible forces will start to dissipate.

On that day, I stopped focusing on the overwhelming data that demonstrates the clear benefits of women being represented at the top: companies are 50 percent more likely to outperform their peers; they create better client retention, organic growth, and profit with gender-balanced teams; and so on. "If this were just about the data," said Tonya, "we would have solved the gender-equity crisis long ago." We need to keep sharing the data, sure, but also connect to the human side of men in power—especially those who want their daughters to have equal opportunity and are likely to become particularly committed and staunch allies, advocates, and co-conspirators in moving the equity conversation forward.

What are we recommending to men? Here are five easy places to start:

1. Encourage women to see themselves as leaders and challenge them when they don't.
2. Welcome women into your peer group to leverage their strengths, not change them.
3. Actively work to evolve the perception of leadership to be more inclusive of women.

4. Sponsor women to be senior leaders by advocating for them behind closed doors.
5. Hire women into executive positions and create the conditions for them to succeed.

We need to acknowledge and encourage the men in our lives who have taken this advice to heart and honor them as shining examples for others to follow. Like with Alan Mulally or the CEO of our auto parts client, I tell their stories publicly and hold them up as role models.

We've now covered the unique hurdles women face on their path to advancement and the critical role organizations play in creating the conditions for women to thrive—specifically focusing on culture, talent systems, leadership development, and executive action. Grounded in this knowledge, our *hope* is that the leadership majority, white men, will embrace the opportunity to become active sponsors in accelerating women's advancement. Our *wish* is that women leaders will become even more discerning when choosing their next role, internally or externally, and actively seek mentors and sponsors who can help them navigate new opportunities. And our *vision* is that organizations will be bold enough to gather the data on how women perceive their organizations so they can continue to attract, engage, and retain even more women leaders.

Women's advancement requires the efforts of all of us.

12

Hope for the Next Generation

We've reached the end of our time together. I hope that you see how committed I am to helping women confront and overcome the hurdles they face as they seek to rise in the corporate world. As the CEO of a company dedicated to changing the face of leadership, my mission is to advance women and other underrepresented groups into leadership roles. But it's more than a professional responsibility; it's a heartfelt passion and core purpose.

I've spent most of this book talking about the challenges women face and how they can overcome them with the support of their organizations. These challenges are real, and they are dire. Even so, as I look to the future, I can't help but feel a sense of hope—and more than a flicker, a brightly glowing flame.

I would never minimize what women have been through. While we are making progress, it hasn't been easy these last several years. Given this reality, it would be understandable to focus on the negative. After all, progress has moved at a glacial pace, and we still have such a very long way to go.

However, I see so many signs that we are moving in the right direction that I can't help but feel encouraged. The corporate spotlight on gender equity and inclusion is brighter than ever, with more organizations making public their aspirations to prioritize this issue and many investors now requiring female board members. These purposeful actions have led to the highest level of women on corporate boards today than at any other point in history, peaking at 29 percent by March 2023.

More than ever before, I am convinced that this is our moment to act. Our job right now is to find those points of light, where things are going well, and amplify them. In the process of doing so, we'll perpetuate more progress.

Much of this book focuses on the women who are leading in the workforce today, mostly Gen X and Gen Y (millennials), as Baby Boomers exit and Gen Z enters. I have a lot of gratitude for the Baby Boomers, who entered the workforce in the 1960s with only two viable options—to become teachers or secretaries. My mom, Sandy Baker, surprised her parents by announcing she planned to go to college to get her teaching degree, even though she already had a "perfectly fine" job as a secretary, with a skill set that included rapid typing and transcribing in shorthand. By the time the end of the Boomers trickled into the workforce, it was the 1980s and much more acceptable for women to aspire to "any" job. However, these were the women who took on the most sexual assault and harassment, overt discrimination and sexism, and the burden of breaking down every barrier as the "first" woman in most professional offices.

My generation, Gen X, started working in the mid-1980s and spent the next 20 years trying to prove ourselves in a corporate setting. We are the generation who experienced every hurdle before we even had words for them, before we understood how high they were, before our organizations even knew they had a role to play in breaking them down.

Gens Y and Z joined the workforce at the turn of the century and will make up more than half the workforce by 2025. We want these women to stand on our shoulders and face the hurdles from a completely different angle than their Gen X predecessors did. We want it—we need it—to be easier for them.

I have so much hope for this next generation of leaders, and I'm counting on both men and women to carry us forward, faster.

EMERGING MEN LEADERS—YOUR RESPONSIBILITY FOR AWARENESS, ALLYSHIP, AND ACTION

Let's start with men in the early stages of their career, who have an opportunity at a much younger age than men in previous generations to explore their biases and develop an awareness of their critical role in history. They can now lead the way by operating inclusively in the world and supporting equity across leadership levels for women and other historically underrepresented populations.

A few weeks after the vice-presidential debate in 2020 and just before the November election, I was in the kitchen with my then 17-year-old son, Will. A senior in high school, he was old enough to have political opinions but hadn't necessarily reflected on the rationale behind them.

"I don't like Kamala Harris," he said.

I asked him why.

He replied, "She seems very aggressive to me."

I took a deep breath, careful not to react. The last thing he wanted from his feminist mother was a lecture.

I casually mentioned the double bind, the idea that women constantly toggle between being likable and being assertive but cannot be seen as both at the same time, unlike men. I told him that throughout history, women leaders have assimilated to the male-dominated leadership style instead of embracing their authenticity.

We looked up the *Harvard Business Review* article titled "Are U.S. Millennial Men Just as Sexist as Their Dads?"[1] and talked about the external biases that had been internalized for both men and women, the biases that cause only 41 percent of millennial men to be comfortable with women being engineers and 43 percent to be comfortable with women as US senators, despite 64 percent of Americans overall having no issue with those feats. The numbers were even lower for the young men's comfort for women being CEOs of Fortune 500 companies (39 percent) or president of the United States (35 percent).

These statistics seemed depressing until the last data points offered a significant evolution from previous generations: millennial men are more likely than previous generations to predict that their wives will have equal careers to theirs and be less likely to do the majority of the childcare. That is cause for hope, but we need to create the time and space to engage young men in this data and in these conversations. We need them to embrace their pivotal role in becoming aware of and overcoming the external biases that still permeate our society.

EMERGING WOMEN LEADERS—
TAKE THE TORCH AND GO FASTER TOGETHER

At this stage of my career, I speak regularly to women across levels and generations in the workforce. In the fall of 2022, I traveled to Dallas to give a keynote at a special women's event at a family-owned real estate investment and development empire. The dynamic CFO entered the workforce as one of the earliest millennials at the turn of the century and has spent the last few decades there as one of the few executive women both in the company and in an industry that lags far behind most in terms of women in leadership. She is the only woman on the investment committee and the HR policy committee.

She realizes her opportunity and responsibility to pave the way for other women, and she told me that for years she has kept in her desk drawer a single yellow Post-it note with the word "WOMEN!" scrawled in thick black pen. She has it there to compel her to support her female employees and colleagues at every turn—fighting for better family benefits, encouraging women to opt into business management roles that put them on the track to the C-suite, and acting as an informal mentor and coach to many women in her firm. It wasn't entirely surprising, then, when she hosted a beautiful event to bring the women together for my keynote speech and an elegant reception to follow.

The women in the room spanned four generations, from Boomers to Gen Z. When it came time for them to ask questions, they fell into predictable categories, with the most interesting comments at the "extremes." Gen X and Gen Y (ensconced in the middle) wanted to know how to ask for and receive feedback, how to help men become more aware of their biases, and how to be more proactive in asking for what they want, from pay to flexibility. The lone Boomer in the room validated how different it was 40 years ago when there was so little opportunity for women. On the other end, the Gen Z women wondered whether their generation would "solve" gender equity, as they had never even heard of the hurdles women face.

The last comment was from a Gen Z woman who oversees intern selection, and she acknowledged that in sifting through hundreds of résumés, she slowly realized that she was holding women to a higher standard. Because she had cleared the high bar to secure a job at this prestigious firm, she wanted to ensure any other woman she recommended would exceed expectations. She asked how she could be sure she wasn't operating from her own unconscious bias.

It all spurred a fantastic dialogue that continued well into the reception.

As I coach and mentor women in college today and introduce the hurdles, I often ask which one resonates the most with them. What I usually find is women at that age just don't know yet which hurdle seems most challenging. Is it because the hurdles don't become more obvious until we're moving through our first several years in a professional environment? Or are the hurdles becoming less significant as each generation of leaders scores higher at supporting women to overcome these hurdles?

We won't know for another 20 years, when Gen Z becomes the leadership majority. In the meantime, we have work to do. Even if we don't individually take up the banner and crusade for more women at the top of the leadership hierarchy, there are plenty of smaller steps we can take. We can go out of our way to support women leaders in our own spheres of influence. We can promote women-led businesses and corporations who express gender equity as a value. We can celebrate small wins, reward and recognize women who are doing well, and share success stories far and wide. Every one of us can build momentum for change and inspire others.

Wherever you are in the world and whatever your organization, your title, or your level—what you do matters. Even our smallest positive actions generate energy that fuels the mighty winds of change.

WHEN WILL WE GET THERE?

The global COVID-19 pandemic created a much deeper awareness of the challenges facing women in the workforce. The shifting public discourse around women and social injustice has created a movement of epic proportions, driving the need for change that starts with open and candid conversations about what it means to live, learn, and lead differently. Despite all the challenges, women remain ambitious: one in three of us aspires to top leadership positions, a figure that has held steady for many years.[2]

It is more important than ever for our organizations—and all of us as leaders—to demonstrate a meaningful commitment to women who have aspirations to lead. And it's time for every woman to reflect on what she wants at this stage in her career and make a commitment to herself to pursue her own development.

Women, you deserve to be in an environment where you are celebrated, not tolerated. A place where you have what you need to grow and thrive. A place where you can operate completely authentically. A place you love. A place that loves you.

ACKNOWLEDGMENTS

For more than 20 years, my father has urged me to write a book. He has an unwavering belief that my story is worth telling and that my experiences are unique. The truth is, we all have a story worth telling, yet most of us don't write a book. But when I became the CEO of Linkage, I realized I could weave my story into a larger context, with proven frameworks and data that provided the necessary foundation and scaffolding. My story—and the stories of other executive women—could now wrap around a singular purpose: to support any woman who aspires to advance in her career, and any organization that aspires to support her.

Dating back more than 30 years when I struck out on my own, I have written annual holiday letters documenting my life lessons. In recent years, my family has gently urged me to stop. They feel that letters folded neatly into holiday cards became passé when we all started mass printing and mailing cards off the internet. They point out that many other families are bypassing all the printing and posting in favor of social media, to save time, money, and the environment. Even so, I can't stop the annual card and letter. Every year I have a message that jumps onto the page. Now, decades in the making, these packages merge to form my life's photo album and journal, documenting my own evolution alongside my family.

I feel the same way about *In Her Own Voice*. It also insisted on being written. I knew I had something to say, and once I finally committed to it, I offered my youngest son Hunter a fee to hold me accountable for writing 10,000 words a month, for six months. He didn't hold up his end of the bargain, but I knew enough to surround myself with a great team and ask for help, because I needed a lot of it. It turns out writing a book is a lot harder than a holiday letter.

I owe an enormous debt of gratitude to Marshall Goldsmith and his 100 Coaches community, who are preeminent authors, speakers, thought leaders, and coaches in the leadership space. They inspired me and opened my eyes to the reality of book writing and publishing. Mostly, they opened their hearts and connections, and helped me see a path forward. Thank you to Scott Osman, Feyzi Fatehi, Rob Nail, Bob Nelson, Chester Elton, Michal Bungay Stanier, Mark Reiter, Elliott Masie, Dorie Clark, Liz Wiseman, Sally Helgesen, and especially Mark Goulston, who ultimately named the book and introduced me to my fabulous editor, Dottie DeHart.

Dottie is my rock, the trusted partner who inserted yellow highlights with insightful comments on each chapter again and again, each time with the right amount of feedback, encouragement, and humor to push me forward. My respect and admiration for Dottie grew over our months together, because I knew she held my vision for this book as tightly as I did, and we challenged each other to deepen our own perspectives and thinking. Dottie kept me going, one word, one page, and one chapter at a time.

Here's what was most surprising about the writing and rewriting process. I rarely go to bed before 11:30 PM, but I knew that to get this book finished, I would need to rise much earlier than my daily 7 AM wakeup. Over the course of a year, without ever setting an alarm, I woke up magically between 5:30 and 5:38 AM, every day of the week. It was as if the Universe was whispering me awake and calling me to my computer for a few hours before the business of the day beckoned. The moment I submitted the first draft of the manuscript and had a six-week author break, I slept soundly again until my 7 AM chimes. The moment I received the manuscript back (this goes on for multiple rounds with the publisher), I reverted to the 5:30 AM schedule, unassisted. For an entire year! That's how I knew

I was operating on purpose; I couldn't have "willed" this to happen. But it wouldn't have happened at all without Dottie.

Scott Miller, it wouldn't have happened without you, either. While neither of us remembers attending Winter Park High School together, many 100 Coaches told me that I must meet you, because your years as an author and speaker at FranklinCovey could inform my plans for the same at Linkage. What an enormous understatement. You took me under your wing, even as you were writing your own books, speaking, podcasting, and starting your literary and speaker's agency. I am grateful that you believed in me enough to pour so much of your hard-earned expertise into texts and Saturday morning phone calls. I will never forget the Park City debacle when our pre-launch social media debut was thwarted by a blizzard, leaving you and Stephanie with multiple bottles of champagne and a pile of your own books that you had wrapped with carefully printed *In Her Own Voice* covers.

There are several ways to publish a book, but I knew I wanted a respected and traditional publisher who could lend credibility and distribution. I heard many warnings about what to expect (and not expect) from a publisher; how to shop the proposal; and how to negotiate the best deal. But when I met Matt Holt at BenBella Books, I shopped no further. His steady voice and calm demeanor helped me believe I could do this. He has built an incredible imprint, Matt Holt Books, with a team of exceptional women who guided our Linkage team through every step. Katie, Brigid, Jessika, Mallory, Kerri, and Ariel—thank you.

Even as I surrounded myself with a team of book professionals, nothing was more important than the Linkage team of experts who held our insight, data, products, and client relationships close. My executive team has been alongside me for the five-year transformation of the company, anchored by our mission to "change the face of leadership." I had to ensure they believed in this book, because it was a Linkage product, and I wouldn't have done it without their support.

Kristen Howe and Shannon Bayer plowed through the first draft with me for many months. They ensured we were reflecting what had changed in the world alongside what had changed in the women's leadership space and in our own research and experience. They brought their ideas, their stories, and their feedback, and their words are intertwined with mine throughout the book. Sarah Breigle brought her marketing expertise to guide our team through the launch plan. Rick Pumfrey carefully negotiated and executed every contract, and Kristin Barrett rounded out the team with her positive reinforcement! We did all this while serving our clients and running a company. And to complicate things further, we were in the middle of an acquisition. In retrospect, trying to write a book at the same time may have been overly ambitious.

I remember the moment I told my team that we needed to think about this book as any other new Linkage product, which required a full launch team, from product management to marketing, project coordination, editorial, and creative design. We gathered a tiger team to push this book across the finish line. Thank you to Melissa Turk, who ensured we met every deadline and attended to every detail; to Barbara Rounds-Smith, who compiled edits from a multitude of readers and read every word of the book many times over; to Lori Hart, who brought her creative design genius; and to Deana LaFauci, who conceptualized the initial marketing and launch plan. It was important to me that this felt like "our" Linkage book, and your contributions along the way made that possible.

Kelly Gruber, you are my professional manager and protector, ensuring that I take care of business and take care of myself. Thank you for your compassionate attention every day. You know all my secrets, and I trust you with them.

We sold the company to SHRM just as we were finishing this manuscript. I couldn't wait to tell Matt at BenBella about the acquisition because of SHRM's vast platform and global reach. With a vision to "build a world of work that works for all," SHRM is the foremost expert, convener, and thought leader on issues impacting today's evolving workplaces. I was overwhelmed by the SHRM team's belief in this book, as evidenced by their immediate support, amplifying anything we could have done on our own. SHRM executives and staff have trusted me to represent this work on every SHRM stage globally, and I will be eternally grateful, especially to Johnny C. Taylor, Jr., Nick Schacht, and Tina Beaty.

And now, to my tribe of sisters who encourage me every day: Thank you to the Visionistas—Simmons, Meg, Amy, and Kirsten—and my other BFFs—Kristi, Kimberly, and Smitha. To the Wine Mamas of SoBe: we've been through a lot together since our kids were in kindergarten. Here's to aging with continued wisdom, grace, and laughter!

My mom, Sandy Baker, is my person, the one who is on the receiving end of the phone almost daily. She has lived every story in this book with me, and her unconditional love propels me. My brother David ranks right up at the top, too. I scored big in the sibling lottery. I'm still sorry that when you called me from the airport to debrief the early book chapters that you left all your brand-new US Open gear at the O'Hare Starbucks—and lost it all.

To my loving and devoted husband, Chip McCollum: When you give me latitude to work too much, you tell the kids that I'm the "hardest-working Mommy in the DMV." I know that's code for, "I've got you covered." Throughout our entire marriage, you have been a true partner, accepting my work as my mission, and gently nudging me toward food or rest when I'm past my prime on any given day. I love you forever.

Thanks also to my dad, Roy Scherer, who read early versions of every chapter and watched every speech, offering nothing but positive reinforcement. Deep down, I know I wrote this book because of your belief in me as an author and speaker. It brings me immense joy to know you are proud of me.

Finally, to Madeleine, Will, and Hunter: You are a core part of my stories as a woman, a leader, and a mother. All parents want their children to be happy—to discover their strengths, their passion, their voice. My hope is that I have set that example for you as you make your own way into the world. You are my everything.

NOTES

INTRODUCTION

1. Emma Hinchliffe, "Women CEOs Run More than 10% of Fortune 500 Companies for the First Time in History," *Fortune,* January 12, 2023, https://fortune.com/2023/01/12/fortune-500-companies-ceos-women-10-percent/.
2. McKinsey & Company, "Women in the Workplace," Lean In, 2022, https://wiw-report.s3.amazonaws.com/Women_in_the_Workplace_2022.pdf.
3. McKinsey & Company, "Women in the Workplace."
4. Ella Ceron, "Your Female Coworker Probably Wants to Quit," Bloomberg, April 26, 2022, https://www.bloomberg.com/news/articles/2022-04-26/deloitte-survey-women-are-burnt-out-and-want-to-quit-their-jobs.
5. McKinsey & Company, "Women in the Workplace."
6. Sundiatu Dixon-Fyle, Kevin Dolan, Dame Vivian Hunt, and Sarah Prince, "Diversity Wins: How Inclusion Matters," McKinsey & Company, May 19, 2020, https://www.mckinsey.com/featured-insights/diversity-and-inclusion/diversity-wins-how-inclusion-matters.
7. Jeremy Schneider, "Are Female CEOs Better than Male CEOs?," Personal Finance Club, May 30, 2022, https://www.personalfinanceclub.com/are-female-ceos-better-than-male-ceos/.
8. Deloitte, "Seventy-Two Percent of Working Americans Surveyed Would or May Consider Leaving an Organization for One They Think Is More Inclusive, Deloitte Poll Finds," PR Newswire, June 7, 2017, https://www.prnewswire.com/news-releases/seventy-two-percent-of-working-americans-surveyed-would-or-may-consider-leaving-an-organization-for-one-they-think-is-more-inclusive-deloitte-poll-finds-300469961.html.
9. Jennifer McCollum, "Opening Keynote" (presentation, Women in Leadership Institute, Orlando, FL, November 1, 2022).

10. McKinsey & Company, "Women in the Workplace."

11. Women Business Collaborative and 50/50 Women on Boards™, "Women Leading Boards April 2022 Special Report," April 3, 2022, https://www.wbcollaborative.org/insights/women-leading-boards-march-2022-special-report-in-partnership-with-50-50-women-on-boards/.

12. Martin Armstrong, "It Will Take Another 136 Years to Close the Global Gender Gap," World Economic Forum, April 12, 2021, https://www.weforum.org/agenda/2021/04/136-years-is-the-estimated-journey-time-to-gender-equality/.

CHAPTER 1

1. National Women's Law Center, "The Lifetime Wage Gap, State by State," National Women's Law Center Page, March 16, 2021, https://nwlc.org/resource/the-lifetime-wage-gap-state-by-state.

2. Sherri Gordon, "What Is the #MeToo Movement?" Very Well Mind, April 24, 2022, https://www.verywellmind.com/what-is-the-metoo-movement-4774817.

3. McKinsey & Company, "Women in the Workplace."

4. Catalyst, "The Double-Bind Dilemma for Women in Leadership," August 2, 2018, https://www.catalyst.org/research/infographic-the-double-bind-dilemma-for-women-in-leadership/.

5. Nigel Chiwaya and Naitian Zhou, "The vice presidential debate by the numbers: Topic, attack and interruption tracker," NBC News, October 7, 2020, https://www.nbcnews.com/politics/2020-election/vice-presidential-debate-2020-topics-data-attacks-n1242442.

6. Brian Schwartz, "Some Biden allies wage a shadow campaign to stop Kamala Harris from becoming vice president," CNBC, July 29, 2020, https://www.cnbc.com/2020/07/29/biden-allies-move-to-stop-kamala-harris-from-becoming-vice-president.html?.

7. John Baldoni, "Kamala Harris: Defusing Ambition as an Obstacle to Women in Power," Forbes, August 12, 2020, https://www.forbes.com/sites/johnbaldoni/2020/08/12/kamala-harris-defusing-ambition-as-an-obstacle-to-women-in-power/?sh=54af06a39b65.

CHAPTER 2

1. Meredith Somers, "Women are less likely than men to be promoted. Here's one reason why," MIT Sloan School of Management, April 12, 2022, https://mitsloan.mit.edu/ideas-made-to-matter/women-are-less-likely-men-to-be-promoted-heres-one-reason-why.

2. Somers, "Women are less likely than men to be promoted."

3. Rebecca A. Clay, "Millions of women have left the workforce. Psychology can help bring them back," American Psychological Association, January 1, 2022, https://www.apa.org/monitor/2022/01/special-workforce-losses.

4. Emily Peck, "Research: College-educated women did not leave labor force during pandemic," Axios, March 25, 2022, https://www.axios.com/2022/03/25/women-college-work-force-covid-pandemic.

5. Nancy F. Clark, "Act Now to Shrink the Confidence Gap," *Forbes*, April 28, 2014, https://www.forbes.com/sites/womensmedia/2014/04/28/act-now-to-shrink-the-confidence-gap/?sh=51eb8e915c41.

6. Katty Kay, Claire Shipman, and JillEllyn Riley, "How to Help Young Girls Keep Their Confidence During Puberty," *Time*, April 20, 2018, https://time.com/5247275/confidence-gap-girls/.

CHAPTER 3

1. Deanne Tockey and Maria Ignatova, "Gender Insights Report: How Women Find Jobs Differently," LinkedIn Talent Solutions, 2019, https://business.linkedin.com/content/dam/me/business/en-us/talent-solutions-lodestone/body/pdf/Gender-Insights-Report.pdf.

CHAPTER 4

1. Kelly Watson and Jodi Detjen, "Removing Self-Imposed Barriers to Success for High Potential Women in the Workplace," Orange Grove Consulting, October 2014, https://orangegroveconsulting.com/wp-content/uploads/2017/01/OG-White-Paper-Removing-Self-Imposed-Barriers-FINAL.compressed.pdf.

2. "Trailblazer Awards: Geena Davis," YouTube Video, posted by "WBCollaborative," September 23, 2022, https://www.youtube.com/watch?v=afXHdrI5Bpc.

3. Geena Davis Institute on Gender in Media, "Gender in Media: The Myths & Facts," https://seejane.org/research-informs-empowers/gender-in-media-the-myths-facts/.

4. Geena Davis Institute on Gender in Media, "Female characters in film and TV motivate women to be more ambitious, more successful, and have even given them the courage to break out of abusive relationships," February 25, 2015, https://seejane.org/gender-in-media-news-release/female-characters-film-tv-motivate-women-ambitious-successful-even-given-courage-break-abusive-relationships-release/.

5. Kari Paul, "Women speak up less in college seminars—here's why that matters," MarketWatch, September 29, 2018, https://www.marketwatch.com/story/women-speak-up-less-in-academic-settings-heres-why-that-matters-2018-09-28.

6. Abigail Johnson Hess, "If you want to be a CEO later, play sports now," CNBC, January 11, 2017, https://www.cnbc.com/2017/01/11/want-to-be-a-ceo-later-play-sports-now.html.

7. Rachael Okerlund, "Why Don't Men Take Paternity Leave?," Parent Map, December 16, 2021, https://www.parentmap.com/article/why-paid-paternity-leave-men-statistics.

CHAPTER 6

1. Jess Huang, Alexis Krivkovich, Ishanaa Rambachan, and Lareina Yee, "For mothers in the workplace, a year (and counting) like no other," McKinsey & Company, May 5, 2021, https://www.mckinsey.com/featured-insights/diversity-and-inclusion/for-mothers-in-the-workplace-a-year-and-counting-like-no-other.

2. Holly Corbett, "The New Unpaid Office Housework for Women: Being DEI Leaders," *Forbes*, September 28, 2021, https://www.forbes.com/sites/hollycorbett/2021/09/28/the-new-unpaid-office-housework-for-women-being-dei-leaders/?sh=469eae256e8d.

3. Lareina Yee, "The 'third shift' matters—and women do more of it," *Fast Company*, October 19, 2021, https://www.fastcompany.com/90687404/the-third-shift-matters-and-women-do-more-of-it.

4. McKinsey & Company, "Women in the Workplace."

5. Amelia Harnish, "Perfectionism and Anxiety: The Problem with Trying to Be Perfect," *Health*, June 1, 2022, https://www.health.com/condition/depression/why-perfectionism-could-be-killing-you.

6. Octavia Raheem, *Gather* (self-pub., 2020).

CHAPTER 7

1. Karen Morley, "Doctor explains how women can overcome imposter syndrome," *CEO Magazine*, April 29, 2022, https://www.theceomagazine.com/opinion/women-imposter-syndrome/.

2. Ruth Gotian, "Why You Earned the Right to Have Imposter Syndrome," *Psychology Today*, April 28, 2021, https://www.psychologytoday.com/us/blog/optimizing-success/202104/why-you-earned-the-right-have-imposter-syndrome?eml.

3. Gotian, "Why You Earned the Right to Have Imposter Syndrome."

4. Christine L. Exley and Judd B. Kessler, "The Gender Gap in Self-Promotion," National Bureau of Economic Research, October 2019, https://www.nber.org/papers/w26345.

5. "The Self-Promotion Gap," Mighty Forces, Southpaw Insights, Upstream Analysis, and Grey Horse Communications, accessed March 9, 2023, https://www.selfpromotiongap.com/home.

6. Jon Henley, "Female-led countries handled coronavirus better, study suggests," *Guardian*, August 18, 2020, https://www.theguardian.com/world/2020/aug/18/female-led-countries-handled-coronavirus-better-study-jacinda-ardern-angela-merkel.

7. Dorie Clark, "How Women Can Develop—and Promote—Their Personal Brand," *Harvard Business Review*, March 2, 2018, https://hbr.org/2018/03/how-women-can-develop-and-promote-their-personal-brand.

CHAPTER 9

1. Morgan Smith, "Women by the numbers in 2022: Share of female Fortune 500 CEOs hits all-time high, but other progress stalls," CNBC, December 20, 2022, https://www.cnbc.com/2022/12/20/2022-in-gender-equality-politics-business-pay-gap.html.

2. Jennifer Dannals et al., "The dynamics of gender and alternatives in negotiation," *Journal of Applied Psychology* 106, no. 11 (2021): 1655–72, doi:10.1037/apl0000867.

3. Kim Elsesser, "Why Women Fall Short in Negotiations (It's Not Lack of Skill)," *Forbes*, January 21, 2021, https://www.forbes.com/sites/kimelsesser/2021/01/21/why-women-fall-short-in-negotiations-its-not-lack-of-skill.

4. Elizabeth L. Campbell and Oliver Hahl, "Stop Undervaluing Exceptional Women," *Harvard Business Review*, July 22, 2022, https://hbr.org/2022/07/stop-undervaluing-exceptional-women.

5. Jennifer McCollum, "Yes, Global 500 Women CEO Numbers Are Lackluster—But Other Hopeful Signs Point to a Brighter Future," Linkage Inc. (blog), August 10, 2022, https://www.linkageinc.com/leadership-insights/yes-global-500-women-ceo-numbers-are-lackluster-but-other-hopeful-signs-point-to-a-brighter-future/.

6. Jennifer McCollum, "There's a Great Wake-up Call Around Women in Leadership. We Need to Answer It," Linkage Inc. (blog), September 27, 2022, https://www.linkageinc.com/leadership-insights/theres-a-great-wake-up-call-around-women-in-leadership-we-need-to-answer-it/.

7. McKinsey & Company, "Women in the Workplace."

CHAPTER 10

1. Kim Elsesser, "New Study Reveals 6 Barriers Keeping Women from High-Power Networking," *Forbes*, June 26, 2019, https://www.forbes.com/sites/kimelsesser/2019/06/26/new-study-reveals-6-barriers-keeping-women-from-high-power-networking.

2. Karl Sabbagh, *Twenty-First Century Jet: The Making and Marketing of the Boeing 777* (New York: Scribner, 1996).

3. Bryce Hoffman, *American Icon: Alan Mulally and the Fight to Save Ford Motor Company* (New York: Crown Business, 2012).

4. Alan Mulally and Sarah McArthur, "A Conversation with Alan Mulally About His 'Working Together'© Strategic, Operational, and Stakeholder-Centered Management System," *Leader to Leader* no. 104 (2022): 7–14, doi:10.1002/ltl.20628.

5. "Why we need more strategic networks and invest in work activities outside our area of expertise," YouTube video, posted by "Herminia Ibarra," April 16, 2015, https://youtu.be/69EmOWG8XT0.

CHAPTER 11

1. Jillian Ihsanullah and Nada Hashmi, "Advancing Women Leaders: Changing the Game for Women in the Workplace," Linkage Inc., 2019, https://www.linkageinc.com/wp-content/uploads/Linkage_Changing_The_Game_For_Women_In_The_Workplace.pdf.

2. McKinsey & Company, "Women in the Workplace."

3. McKinsey & Company, "Women in the Workplace."

4. Deana LaFauci, "Getting Started—Executive Sponsorship—What Is It and Who Benefits?," Linkage Inc. (blog), February 4, 2022, https://www.linkageinc.com/leadership-insights/getting-started-executive-sponsorship-what-is-it-and-who-benefits/.

CHAPTER 12

1. Andrea S. Kramer and Alton B. Harris, "Are U.S. Millennial Men Just as Sexist as Their Dads?," *Harvard Business Review*, June 15, 2016, https://hbr.org/2016/06/are-u-s-millennial-men-just-as-sexist-as-their-dads.

2. Yee, "The 'third shift' matters."

Jennifer McCollum
CEO of Linkage, a SHRM Company

Author of
**In Her Own Voice:
A Woman's Rise to CEO**

Jennifer McCollum grew up in an entrepreneurial home in Germany. This unique childhood not only instilled in her grit, resourcefulness, and an iron-clad work ethic—she describes herself as "a hustler by 15"—but also a desire to help others like her access their full potential. Today, she's on a mission to help talented women rise to higher and higher positions of leadership… and to help organizations create cultures where they can excel and thrive.

The winding road she's traveled has led to her current position as CEO of Linkage, a SHRM company, where she oversees the strategic direction and global operations of this leadership development firm. With a mission to "Change the Face of Leadership," Linkage has dedicated more than 35 years to advance women and accelerate inclusion in leaders and organizations. Linkage has been consistently ranked a top 20 training company worldwide, providing assessments, training, coaching, consulting, and conferences.

Jennifer is an acclaimed speaker, consultant, coach, and author, with two decades of experience leading and building businesses in the leadership space. Her expertise includes how to close the gap to gender equity; why the most effective leaders are inclusive leaders; and how to demystify inclusion for leaders and organizations. She has delivered workshops, keynotes, webinars, and podcasts to thousands of leaders globally on live and virtual stages. She is a member of the Marshall Goldsmith 100 Coaches community.

Prior to Linkage, Jennifer spent a decade growing businesses within Korn Ferry and Corporate Executive Board (CEB), now Gartner. At CEB, she led product management within the leadership division, driving innovative solutions that helped organizations select, develop, and place leaders at all levels. She also ran CEB's Leadership Academies business, which developed more than 30,000 professionals in 2,100 companies throughout 50 countries.

Jennifer has a master's degree in communications from the University of Stirling in Stirling, Scotland, and an undergraduate degree in psychology and communications from Wake Forest University. An avid tennis player and skier, she is the mother of three and lives in the Washington, DC, area with her husband.

 jenniferscherermccollum    jennifermccollum   jennifersmccollum

More Ways to *Accelerate* Women in Leadership

Supercharge Your *Individual* Leadership Journey

ATTEND

Women in Leadership Institute™

This immersive leadership conference accelerates women across all levels, industries, and roles, and provides life-changing networking opportunities.

ASSESS

Women's Leadership Assessment

Which hurdles are most challenging to you? Take a complimentary assessment to help you find the answer now—and track your progress.

Empower Women in Your *Organization*

BOOK

Keynote with the Author

Motivate your women leaders, male allies, and executives with Jennifer's interactive keynotes, available in person or virtually.

DISCOVER

Leadership Development Offerings

Linkage's Advancing Women Leaders™ solution enables organizations to attract, retain, develop, and advance women leaders at all levels.

Learn more at SHRM.org/InHerOwnVoice

About Linkage

Linkage, a SHRM company, is a global leadership development firm committed to advancing women and accelerating inclusion in leaders and organizations, trusted by more than 250 clients across industries. For more than 35 years, Linkage has been **changing the face of leadership** by impacting organizational effectiveness and equity. Through our work with more than one million leaders, we continue to evolve our unique datasets, insights, and innovative products to create comprehensive solutions—empowering top organizations to solve their most pressing talent challenges.

Learn more at linkageinc.com.

About SHRM

SHRM creates better workplaces where employers and employees thrive together. As the voice of all things work, workers, and the workplace, SHRM is the foremost expert, convener, and thought leader on issues impacting today's evolving workplaces. With nearly 325,000 members in 165 countries, SHRM impacts the lives of more than 235 million workers and families globally.

Learn more at SHRM.org and on Twitter @SHRM.